Library Technology
REPORTS
Expert Guides to Library Systems and Services

Privacy and Freedom of Information in 21st-Century Libraries

*The ALA Office for Intellectual Freedom,
Jason Griffey, Sarah Houghton-Jan, and Eli Neiburger*

ALA TechSource
alatechsource.org

American Library Association

Library Technology REPORTS

ALA TechSource purchases fund advocacy, awareness, and accreditation programs for library professionals worldwide.

Volume 46, Number 8
Privacy and Freedom of Information in 21st Century Libraries
ISBN: 978-0-8389-5814-8

American Library Association
50 East Huron St.
Chicago, IL 60611-2795 USA
www.alatechsource.org
800-545-2433, ext. 4299
312-944-6780
312-280-5275 (fax)

Advertising Representative
Brian Searles, Ad Sales Manager
ALA Publishing Dept.
bsearles@ala.org
312-280-5282
1-800-545-2433, ext. 5282

Editor
Dan Freeman
dfreeman@ala.org
312-280-5413

Copy Editor
Judith Lauber

Editorial Assistant
Megan O'Neill
moneill@ala.org
800-545-2433, ext. 3244
312-280-5275 (fax)

Production and Design
Tim Clifford, Production Editor
Karen Sheets de Gracia, Manager of Design and Composition

Library Technology Reports (ISSN 0024-2586) is published eight times a year (January, March, April, June, July, September, October, and December) by American Library Association, 50 E. Huron St., Chicago, IL 60611. It is managed by ALA TechSource, a unit of the publishing department of ALA. Periodical postage paid at Chicago, Illinois, and at additional mailing offices. POSTMASTER: Send address changes to Library Technology Reports, 50 E. Huron St., Chicago, IL 60611.

Trademarked names appear in the text of this journal. Rather than identify or insert a trademark symbol at the appearance of each name, the authors and the American Library Association state that the names are used for editorial purposes exclusively, to the ultimate benefit of the owners of the trademarks. There is absolutely no intention of infringement on the rights of the trademark owners.

ALA TechSource
alatechsource.org

Copyright ©2010 American Library Association
All Rights Reserved.

Abstract

This issue of *Library Technology Reports*, conceived and coordinated by the American Library Association's (ALA) Office for Intellectual Freedom, focuses on current topics and concerns around the intersections of technology, security, and intellectual freedom in libraries. As libraries increasingly move beyond the provision of print material and into their expanding roles as providers of digital resources and services, intellectual freedom concerns have been magnified as they apply to a range of complex new issues.

A number of prominent library professionals contributed their expertise for this issue. Authors and topics include Barbara M. Jones on Libraries, Technology and the Culture of Privacy; Eli Neiburger on User-Generated Content; Sarah Houghton-Jan on Internet Filtering; Jason Griffey on Social Networking and the Library; and Deborah Caldwell-Stone on RFID in Libraries.

Subscriptions

alatechsource.org/subscribe

Table of Contents

Chapter 1—Introduction   5
By Angela Maycock
- Notes   7

Chapter 2—Libraries, Technology, and the Culture of Privacy   8
By Barbara M. Jones
- Vastly Different Legal and Regulatory Environments   9
- Different Levels of National Technological Development   9
- Different Cultural Interpretations for the Meaning of Privacy   10
- Clash of Priorities and Values—Transparency versus Privacy   11
- Recommendations   11
- Notes   12

Chapter 3—User-Generated Content   13
By Eli Neiburger
- Ownership and Copyright   14
- Responsibility and Privacy   16
- Exposure and Risk   18
- Licenses and Terms of Use   20
- The Bottom Line: Reality for Modern Libraries   23

Chapter 4—Internet Filtering   25
By Sarah Houghton-Jan
- Laws and Court Cases Related to Internet Filters   25
- Technology of Filters   26
- Filter Accuracy   27
- Privacy and Filters   27
- Intellectual Freedom and Filters   28
- Additional Library Challenges with Filtering   29
- Conclusion   31
- Notes   31
- Resources for Further Information   32

Chapter 5—Social Networking and the Library   34
By Jason Griffey
- Notes   37

Chapter 6—RFID in Libraries   38
By Deborah Caldwell-Stone
- Overview   38
- A Controversy in Libraryland   39
- The Library Community Responds   39
- Privacy Concerns Inherent in RFID Applications   39
- Professional Ethics and Privacy-Invading Technologies   40
- Privacy Guidelines and Consensus   41
- NISO Offers A New Model for RFID in Libraries   41
- Conclusion   42
- Notes   43

About the Authors   45

Chapter 1

Introduction

Angela Maycock

Abstract

This chapter of Privacy and Freedom of Information in 21st-Century Libraries *provides a backdrop for the entire issue. As libraries increasingly move beyond the provision of print material and into their expanding roles as providers of digital resources and services, intellectual freedom concerns have been magnified as they apply to a range of complex new issues.*

This issue of *Library Technology Reports*, conceived and coordinated by the American Library Association's (ALA) Office for Intellectual Freedom, focuses on current topics and concerns around the intersections of technology, security, and intellectual freedom in libraries. This territory offers a wide range of opportunities for insight and commentary, as these issues encompass some of the most pressing, and sometimes distressing, challenges facing libraries today. A group of thoughtful and articulate library leaders have contributed chapters to this publication, bringing diverse perspectives to both technology's applications in libraries and librarians' professional values and ethics. Our goals with this publication are to bring together current research, thought, and experience around the issues at hand; to stimulate discussion and the development of new ideas; and to share a range of both theoretical and practical approaches to our shared dilemmas.

Librarians, in some cases, may intuitively consider intellectual freedom principles in a context of print-based technologies. For example, libraries' observance of Banned Books Week—celebrating the freedom to read and drawing attention to the harms of censorship by highlighting actual or attempted removals of books across the United States—extends back to 1982. However, just as our users' reading and intellectual pursuits have extended into new media, our intellectual freedom concerns as librarians have long ago expanded well beyond the realm of book censorship alone. As libraries increasingly move beyond provision of print material and into their expanding roles as providers of digital resources and services, intellectual freedom concerns have been magnified as they apply to a range of complex new issues.

Yet the foundation for our professional values and concerns remains the same, even as specific technologies and the challenges they pose to libraries have changed and will continue to evolve. The *Library Bill of Rights*, first adopted in 1939, identifies libraries as "forums for information and ideas" and serves as the American Library Association's foundational statement on intellectual freedom in libraries.[1] The basic formula for intellectual freedom requires only two essential conditions: freedom of expression and access to information. Libraries fulfill a unique role in this equation through their mission of providing access to all points of view on the issues of our times and through their commitment to making those ideas and opinions available to anyone who needs or wants them.

The *Library Bill of Rights* serves as an aspirational document, stating libraries' basic values to guide the provision of services and development of policy. In order to meet the need for more practical advice, the ALA's Intellectual Freedom Committee has developed numerous Interpretations to the *Library Bill of Rights*, which concern themselves with the application of its principles to specific library situations. Readers of *Library Technology Reports* may be particularly interested in new and recently revised Interpretations on topics such as "Minors and Internet Interactivity" and "Access to Digital Information, Services, and Networks" that provide policy frameworks for decisions related to digital resources in libraries. All Interpretations and many other resources from ALA's *Intellectual Freedom Manual* are now organized and available online.

Intellectual Freedom Manual
www.ifmanual.org

Internet access has established itself as by far the most significant and transformative digital service in a majority of American libraries today. The ALA Office for Library Advocacy notes that public libraries have become "the number one point of online access for people without Internet connections at home, school, or work" and that an overwhelming 98.7 percent of public libraries provide public access to the Internet.[2] In addition, as of 2009, "almost 73 percent of libraries report they are the only source of free access to computers and the Internet in their communities."[3] Libraries of all types are now focusing more and more of their efforts and expenditures on the provision of adequate Internet access to meet patrons' growing needs.

Over the past several years, as the economic environment has grown more difficult and disheartening, our country's libraries—always accustomed to doing more with less—have found their budgets slashed as usage has simultaneously soared. People today are flocking to libraries as sources of information and entertainment in record numbers, and one of the greatest strains on libraries' stretched resources has been in the area of Internet access. The economic downturn has caused patrons to demand increased access to online content in order to apply for jobs, access e-government tools, take advantage of continuing education opportunities, and more.

In addition, the Internet's role as a vehicle for ideas, entertainment, collaboration, and dialogue is itself expanding rapidly. Internet users are no longer simply passive recipients of information, but active creators as well, interacting with the content they encounter online and adding their own content in response. This astounding proliferation of user-generated material takes the form of text, images, videos, podcasts, and much more. Libraries, by providing Internet access to users, can now extend the richness and depth of existing resources by connecting users with this wealth of content alongside our own array of traditional collections and services. Articles by Jason Griffey and Eli Neiburger in this publication consider the specific implications of user-generated content and social networking tools in the library and the vital questions of access, ownership, privacy, and policies that such usage entails.

At the same time that school, public, academic, and other libraries are encountering such unprecedented new opportunities for providing access to ideas, a multitude of concerns have arisen around the Internet's much-touted potential. Some individuals and groups strongly believe that the Internet simply provides too much access—especially for young people, but often for adults as well—to potentially offensive, inappropriate, or even dangerous material online. What many see as enhanced capabilities for sharing and communication on the Internet are viewed by others as endangering child safety by opening the door to increased or unmonitored interactions with strangers. Others, including many librarians, are also concerned about issues such as the Internet's vast swaths of unreliable or inaccurate information and the many ways in which personal privacy can be compromised when taking advantage of ever-expanding resources online.

In the library context, all of these concerns must be balanced with equally compelling concerns about free and open access to ideas. Our shared values and ethics provide our profession with a basic framework, but in addition, all publicly funded libraries have a legal obligation to provide access to constitutionally protected information. Internet filters and other barriers to access present a number of complex legal, technical, and ethical issues. Sarah Houghton-Jan's article addresses such issues, ranging from laws and court cases to intellectual freedom and accuracy, in grappling with libraries' difficult filtering decisions. The article's emphasis on the library's role in educating the community on both technology and intellectual freedom concerns is a theme that echoes throughout this issue.

Another theme to be found throughout the articles in this issue is the importance of strong library policy in meeting the challenges posed by technology and intellectual freedom head on. "Written policies can emphasize the library's support for the principles of intellectual freedom and its respect for the diversity of its community while at the same time establishing that the library does not condone the use of its computers to access materials that are obscene or otherwise illegal."[4] Policies should address reasonable time, place, or manner restrictions in determining the use of digital services and resources. Clear, written policies, based on institutional objectives and combined with strong support for intellectual freedom principles, form a solid foundation for the library's decision making around specific technologies and their applications.

As libraries of all types find themselves treading this difficult ground, our decision making should also be informed by active discussion, deliberation, and collaboration with our colleagues and peers. Yet barriers may exist to this level of engaged and informed dialogue even within our own profession. A dual focus on intellectual freedom issues and technology issues alongside one another is surprisingly rare in the professional literature today. Too often, intellectual freedom is given only short shrift in critical commentary on libraries' choices and uses of technology. Similarly, in-depth consideration of specific technologies and their applications may tend to fall by the wayside when library authors focus on vital issues around our core value of intellectual freedom. Some of librarianship's best and brightest thinkers focus their research and writing on either technology or intellectual freedom issues. Yet why do we see so little inquiry that bridges the divide between the two?

When forward-thinking, tech-oriented librarians write about evaluating emerging technologies, the focus often tends to be on practical issues like pricing, implementation, and sustainability. These crucial concerns should be paired with serious consideration of how such technologies impact users' rights and how they may or may not line up with our professional values. When intellectual freedom advocates write about our professional values in practice, the conclusions often tend toward the abstract or overbroad. Librarians on the front lines need thoughtful consideration of specific technologies, their practical applications, and viable solutions to the choices and trade-offs we confront. Libraries' use of radio frequency identification (RFID) technology, addressed here in an article by Deborah Caldwell-Stone, is one example of an issue where tech librarians and intellectual freedom fighters have each been examining the questions and concerns at hand but, for too long, have been speaking on different channels from one another.

Part of our aim with this issue of *Library Technology Reports* is to begin to remedy this situation. By presenting analysis from intellectual freedom leaders alongside that from some of our most active and thoughtful technology advocates, we hope to open up lines of communication, to invite one another into our separate spheres, and to ensure that our thinking and our conclusions are better informed by the insights of one other. More involved and ongoing dialogue is needed, and the articles in this publication should help to lead the way.

Intellectual freedom, in order to remain a vibrant and central aspect of not only the theory but the practice of librarianship, must be infused in all that we do. This extends naturally to libraries' use of technology, which, in order to truly fulfill the goals and missions of our institutions, must be informed by all of our most basic and central professional values. As we navigate user wants and needs, libraries must keep one eye on useful, creative technological solutions while focusing the other on upholding intellectual freedom. We want to take advantage of opportunities to engage our library users and allow them to connect with the library while also protecting their rights. We ought to embrace our role in educating patrons, not only in traditional areas like search strategies and basic technology skills, but also on topics more broadly related to library values like safe and responsible Internet use or protecting their privacy online.

At the same time, during an economic downturn, libraries recognize that sacrifices are necessary. In determining what technology we are able offer to our users and how, trade-offs are inevitable. Libraries today serve increasingly diverse populations, and we also face challenges around the global nature of information, a topic that Barbara Jones considers in depth in her contribution to this publication. "As the free flow of information transcends national boundaries, it becomes increasingly clear that prohibitions on freedom of expression in one country will inhibit the freedom of those in many other countries around the world."[5] While libraries continue to struggle to fulfill their missions and meet user needs under ever more difficult conditions, we must remain mindful of our responsibility to serve our patrons with integrity and good faith.

In the face of vexing technological concerns, librarians also have a responsibility to be critical. As a profession, we are well served by both our skepticism and our ability to stay informed on topics of vital concern to libraries and patrons alike. Librarians must remain alert to the dilemmas that face us in reconciling our uses of technology with our professional integrity. The changes that have brought us to this point are substantial but have not shaken, and will not diminish, our commitment to librarianship's core values. As new technologies continue their inexorable advance, "libraries are changing not what we do, but how we do it. . . . The principles, however, remain the same. Our role, then, is to navigate these changes, protect our principles and values and continue to make sure that our users have the ideas and the information that they need when they need them."[6]

Notes

1. American Library Association, *Library Bill of Rights*, adopted June 19, 1939; amended Oct. 14, 1944; June 18, 1948; Feb. 2, 1961; June 27, 1967; and Jan. 23, 1980; www.ala.org/ala/issuesadvocacy/intfreedom/librarybill/index.cfm (accessed Aug. 9, 2010).
2. ALA Office for Library Advocacy, *Quotable Facts about America's Libraries* (Chicago: American Library Association, 2010).
3. Larra Clark and Denise Davis, "The State of Funding for Library Technology in Today's Economy," *Library Technology Reports* 45, no. 1 (Jan. 2009): 6.
4. ALA Office for Intellectual Freedom, *Intellectual Freedom Manual*. 8th ed. (Chicago: American Library Association, 2010), 40.
5. Ibid., xviii.
6. Judith Krug, "Introduction," in Barbara M. Jones *Libraries, Access, and Intellectual Freedom: Developing Policies for Public and Academic Libraries* (Chicago: American Library Association, 1999), xviii.

Chapter 2

Libraries, Technology, and the Culture of Privacy

A Global Perspective

Barbara M. Jones

Abstract

The International Federation of Library Associations (IFLA) views privacy as integral to freedom of expression, as stated in its Internet Manifesto, *and in its* Guidelines. *The international stage is set for librarians to consider privacy as a professional core value extending to technological applications in libraries. This chapter of* Privacy and Freedom of Information in 21st-Century Libraries *examines the legal, technological, cultural and practical implications of protecting intellectual freedom in the global age.*

This chapter is not a scholarly analysis of the stated topic, though there is opportunity for important work there. Rather, it is a set of observations based on my teaching the *Internet Manifesto* curriculum to librarians in Africa, Latin America, and East Asia. That curriculum, devised by the International Federation of Library Associations' Committee on Free Access to Information and Freedom of Expression (FAIFE), is heavily based on Article 19 of the United Nations' *Universal Declaration of Human Rights*, but also on Article 12: "No one shall be subjected to arbitrary or unlawful interference with his privacy, family, home, or correspondence, nor to unlawful attacks on his honour and reputation."[1]

The International Federation of Library Associations (IFLA) views privacy as integral to freedom of expression, as stated in its *Internet Manifesto*, and in its *Guidelines*:

User Privacy
- Librarians must respect the privacy of Internet users in the library and their information seeking choices.
- Librarians should keep no more record of Internet use than is required by law, retain such records no longer than is required, and protect the integrity of records at all times.[2]

So the international library profession has committed itself, via written policy, to library user privacy and in extending that privacy to Internet access. The legendary U.S. Supreme Court Justice Thurgood Marshall put it this way in regard to reader privacy: "If the First Amendment means anything, it means that a state has no business telling a man, sitting alone in his house, what books he may read or what films he may watch."[3]

Thus the international stage is set for librarians to consider privacy as a professional core value extending to technological applications in libraries. In fact, over thirty national library associations (from Armenia to Japan to Malaysia to Mexico to the Russian Federation) have included privacy, if not a reference to technology, in their codes of ethics.[4]

But it is one thing for a group to espouse a common professional idea—which does not have the force of law—and another to apply these best practices in individual countries with unique political cultures. And there is increasing concern within IFLA that many of its core documents reflect the Western tradition of freedom of expression and privacy. This concern is reflected in the current scholarly discourse over the inequities of globalization (see such journals as *Perspectives on Global Development and Technology*, published by Brill). Here are some of the barriers to libraries embracing privacy in the technological environment:

- vastly different legal and regulatory environments
- different levels of national technological development

- different cultural interpretations for the meaning of privacy
- clash of priorities and values—transparency versus privacy

Vastly Different Legal and Regulatory Environments

A publicly funded library is usually subject to privacy laws and regulations at its country's national, local, and state levels—and to regional and international agreements, some of which are nonbinding. National library associations should assume the responsibility for collecting these laws and understanding their applicability to library patron data. In the United States, as an example, there is no explicit right to privacy in the U.S. Constitution. The approach is, rather, sectoral, meaning that different bodies of law are developed for different sectors—such as health care, educational institutions, and so on. Library user privacy could conceivably be influenced by the following laws, regulations, and agreements:

- National legislative protections such as the 1986 Electronic Communications Privacy Act and, in contrast, the setbacks to privacy in the 2001 USA PATRIOT Act.
- Regulatory agency actions. For example, the Federal Communications Commission has taken the lead in protecting consumers from private sector misuse of personally identifiable information.
- Constitutional protections. For example, Katz v. U.S. protects people from government eavesdropping as prohibited by the Fourth Amendment.
- State laws, such as the library confidentiality statutes or agreements in each state. Information on state privacy laws is available on the ALA website.
- International agreements such as the Organisation for Economic Co-operation and Development (OECD) Guidelines of 1980, which protect privacy and transborder flows of personal data.

State Privacy Laws Regarding Library Records
www.ala.org/ala/aboutala/offices/oif/ifgroups/stateifc chairs/stateifcinaction/stateprivacy.cfm

The United States government, like most, tries to strike a balance between promoting the individual's right to privacy and protecting national security. Many civil society groups argue that the balance has tipped too far toward national security and surveillance with the passage of the USA PATRIOT Act in 2001, which trumps state laws governing confidentiality of library records, and the 2006 extension of the 1994 Communications Assistance for Law Enforcement Act (CALEA), which allows surveillance of the Internet.

The European Union, on the other hand, is subject to the 1995 European Union Data Protection Directive. It is a very strong set of directives—so strong that special negotiations were necessary before the EU would allow data transfers into the United States. (U.S. data privacy regulations are much weaker than the EU mandates.)

Most countries in the developing world, in contrast, have very few privacy laws, regulations, or directives. The just-released *IFLA World Report 2010* shows that, of the 122 countries responding (the report is usually submitted by the national librarian or head of the national library association), only 17 reported national antiterror legislation "that affects Intellectual Freedom." (Further research by the report's compilers found far more antiterrorism legislation than was reported.) Sadly, only one half of the 122 respondents had any opinion about the legislation's impact on reader privacy. And of the seventeen countries reporting they have antiterror legislation, only five elaborated on the negative impact: the United States, the United Kingdom, Japan, Italy, and the Netherlands. These results clearly demonstrate that privacy is not on the radar screens of many librarians—at least those who responded to the survey. Regarding the survey question about whether libraries keep patron usage records, the compilers concluded there was not enough data to make valid deductions by region. However, of the respondents to the question "whether keeping usage records affects freedom of access to information of the individual Internet library user," 66.7 percent of European libraries said yes; 66.7 percent of African librarians responded no. I am writing this article at the 2010 IFLA Conference in Gothenburg, Sweden, and I can confirm from conversations and the dearth of presentations that library privacy is not on the agenda—particularly in the developing world. As one national librarian of an African country told me, "Most of us are so focused on obtaining computers and bandwidth that Internet privacy is not an issue we have the luxury of discussing."

IFLA World Report 2010
http://ifla-world-report.org

Different Levels of National Technological Development

Much has been written about the "digital divide," and indeed it is a key factor in barriers to Internet access for all. The *IFLA World Report 2010* collected information about library Internet access from 122 countries. In terms of Internet access in public libraries worldwide, only 37.3 percent of reporting countries have 81-100 percent of their public libraries with Internet access. In Africa, there is only one country with public libraries at that level—Egypt; in Latin America, 10 out of 22. These results are only slightly higher than the 2007 report, so the developing world is experiencing little movement toward public library Internet access.

One third of African countries reported that only 20 percent or fewer of their university libraries have Internet access—the same as the 2007 report. To put this digital divide in higher education in context, 80 percent of the reporting countries have Internet access in 61-100 percent of university libraries. But 15 countries are at the level of 40 percent to less than 20 percent—and 8 of these 15 are in Africa.

Here is another way to dramatize the problem: of the 122 countries reporting, 4 countries report that less than 20 percent of libraries in each category—academic, school, and public—have Internet access. All these low statistics come from Africa. No countries in Europe, Latin American, or North America report any type of library in that lowest category of 20 percent Internet access. It is easy to see why African countries aren't thinking of privacy at the moment—even though, arguably, it is best to incorporate privacy safeguards at the very beginning of building technological infrastructure.

These discouraging statistics also mean that many countries have not yet developed a national information infrastructure. Those governments' decision makers have not directly experienced the value of Web 2.0 and other technology for public policy work. Library and IT staff in those countries do not have workplace access to computers and the Internet. At a recent library meeting in the developing world, my colleague turned to me and said, "Most of the librarians in this room can't turn on a computer, because they didn't have them in library school and they don't have them in their libraries." Nor do they do have access to technology training programs or experience with user services and interfaces. At FAIFE's first *Internet Manifesto* workshop (2006 in Central America), my colleague was demonstrating how she trains users and promotes YouTube and Facebook in her U.S. urban public library. She was met with blank stares. We learned very quickly not to take anything for granted. While it is important to demonstrate innovation, it is also important to know the audience's frame of reference. There was simply no way that she could explain the privacy issues surrounding Facebook to that audience on that occasion.

In 2009 I presented a two-day invitational workshop in an African country to help government ministry officials and librarians adopt social media for government websites in order to encourage citizen participation and interaction. I was unable to show examples from such interesting United States government agency websites as www.whitehouse.gov or www.fema.gov because the Internet bandwidth was too slow. This was a frustrating example of a government that could not implement its vision of citizen participation in e-government because it put the social media cart before the bandwidth horse. And of course, privacy concerns were not on the radar screen at all.

Different Cultural Interpretations for the Meaning of Privacy

While attending a conference in Oslo, I asked a library colleague whether librarians' salaries were sufficient to accommodate the extremely high cost of living. He—hardly a close friend—casually revealed to me his exact salary. In Norway and other socialist-leaning countries, one's salary is not considered as private as it is in the United States. Anthropologists and other researchers are finding that the concepts of privacy and "personal sphere" differ from culture to culture. Further, some cultures determine that certain actions are not decided by individual citizens because the individual has a moral obligation to act on behalf of the larger community. And in most societies some actions are based on gender roles.

But one concept seems universal. Clinical studies across cultures seem to indicate that "there are basic psychological limits to the extent to which others (including society) can impinge on the private lives of individuals."[5] And "[w]hat is being recognized is that basic requirements for psychological integrity include the establishment of an arena of personal choice and privacy."[6] But cultural definitions and norms may differ; nonetheless, this sphere does exist to an extent. This includes children and adolescents. This research applies to children of various ages and leads to important questions about how much privacy and agency should be afforded to young people as part of their development.

It is important to underscore that in all cultures, people do seem to care about a certain modicum of personal privacy. In many countries in which HIV/AIDS is a large public health concern, librarians report that in small villages or towns, clinic workers will not keep the blood test results confidential. As a result many librarians in the developing world have experienced patrons consulting the library about HIV/AIDS instead of the clinic. One African colleague stayed in the same hospital room with a pregnant HIV/AIDS patient who was not told how pregnancy with HIV/AIDS should be dealt with. After her release, the librarian did research and returned to the hospital room to relay the information to the pregnant woman, who trusted her over the hospital workers.

I am not making the argument that human rights are culturally relative. In fact, Nucci says, "Empirical work indicates that there is both evidence for a psychological basis for claims to basic human rights, and considerable contextual and cultural variation in their expression."[7] However, for the real world of library Internet access and service, the great human rights documents and the word *privacy* must be translated into practical applications.

Clash of Priorities and Values—Transparency versus Privacy

E-government is, in most cases, a well-intentioned and promising way for governments to collect public records and, in some cases, aggregate them and make them available online so that citizens can monitor government accountability and accessibility.

The "one card" or "universal ID" has become an integral element of many e-government services. Some countries are developing cards so that citizens can do anything from paying their water bill, to checking out library books, to consulting a local health clinic for an HIV/AIDS status update. Much government business can be transacted at centrally located kiosks. The clash of equally compelling values was made clear to me during a workshop on the *Internet Manifesto* in Central America. When I asked my colleagues whether they were concerned about having so much personal information on one chip, they replied that fighting corruption (not to mention personal convenience) outweighed their concerns over personal privacy. Before the "one card," it often took over four hours to pay a utility bill or transact government business. Thus many people were compelled to pay workers to stand in line for them. This system bred corruption. Local public employee unions opposed these cards because the kiosks took away their jobs. In evaluating what the developed world calls "progress," we must look at the local complexities and decide how to promote privacy when it is not a high priority or is a conflicting value.

Novelist and rights activist Henning Mankell tells the story about his conversation with young street boys in Mozambique. When asked what they wanted more than anything in the world, they told him, "A national identity card so that people know who I am." Only after he asked them how they would get a card did they mention the importance of being able to read and write.[8] And so, when we librarians in the developed world tell librarians in the developing world that they must move privacy to the top of their list of professional values, we must listen to the reasons why it isn't there now.

Recommendations

I am persuaded by the approach of such thinkers as Helen Nissenbaum in her 2010 book, *Privacy in Context: Technology, Policy, and the Integrity of Social Life*.[9] Although her book and approach focus mostly to the United States, I believe that her conclusions and theories could be applied to privacy solutions in a global context. Nissenbaum asserts that legal and political structures might not be the best way to promote privacy. Instead, she suggests that we (1) look at information flow in our culture; (2) identify places in which lack of privacy has disrupted the integrity of our lives; and (3) address and solve the problem by fixing the information flow. The problem might be fixed via laws, but we don't start with a law and point it at the problem; we start with the problem and devise the proper legal or regulatory fixes. This approach is relevant for non-U.S. libraries, where each country's history, legal structure, and cultural norms will define the private sphere differently; therefore, the libraries need a variety of options for fixing the invasion of privacy. While I view the rule of law and such documents as the *Universal Declaration of Human Rights* as essential, they are too vague for practical library application.

I would make the following recommendations:

- The national library association should collect, make available, and monitor national legislation and international treaties by which its country is bound—and determine how they apply to libraries.
- The national library association should adopt a code of ethics with privacy embedded therein.
- Librarians should share ideas about how to present the right to privacy in a dramatic way. Here at the Gothenburg IFLA conference, I realized that slides of the burning of Harry Potter books are far more emotionally compelling than abstract notions of personal data theft. How do we envision privacy and tell the story? Elementary schools students told me we should act it out in plays. Others recommend posters with colorful, catchy slogans. The American Library Association Privacy Revolution uses an edgy video. Maybe showing and discussing movies like *The Lives of Others* would make a more emotional impact.

Privacy Revolution
www.privacyrevolution.org

- Librarians should work closely with legislators to help fashion laws that address privacy protection.
- Employers should train librarians and IT professionals about the principles of privacy, as outlined in the Code of Fair Information Practices.
- Librarians worldwide should avoid reinventing the wheel by consulting the privacy policy formulations of such organizations as IFLA/FAIFE and the American Library Association's Office for Intellectual Freedom.

- Libraries should not attempt to promote privacy by banning social media. Rather, they should teach library users how to use it responsibly.
- Librarians should find ways to show how the loss of privacy is incremental. I am reminded of an exhibit at the Museum of the Resistance in Amsterdam. This exhibit documents how the Jews of Amsterdam lost certain rights one by one. First they could not order telephones. Next they could not be on the street during certain hours. Then they were restricted to certain areas of the city. Because the restrictions were introduced over a period of years, they were easier to tolerate. Many believe that the loss of privacy happens in the same way and that the result can also be catastrophic. Another analogy is the development of the system of apartheid in South Africa, in which all citizens were categorized into one of eleven racial/ethnic groups. This data was stored on a computer. In fact, much of our history documents oppression enforced by taking away the private sphere of the individual victims.
- We should listen to librarians who (1) have lived in repressive regimes, (2) live in countries with no privacy protections, and (3) believe that privacy is gone and that we should get over it. While we may disagree with some of their approaches, we can't address the problem without the benefit of their wisdom.

Notes

1. UN General Assembly, *Universal Declaration of Human Rights*, Dec. 10, 1948, available online at www.un.org/en/documents/udhr (accessed Aug. 30, 2010).
2. IFLA/FAIFE, *IFLA/UNESCO Internet Manifesto Guidelines* (The Hague, Netherlands: IFLA, Sept. 2006), 25, www.ifla.org/files/faife/publications/policy-documents/internet-manifesto-guidelines-en.pdf (accessed Aug. 30, 2010).
3. Thurgood Marshall, Opinion of the Court, *Stanley v. Georgia* (394 U.S 557 [1969]).
4. IFLA, "Professional Codes of Ethics for Librarians," March 18, 2010, www.ifla.org/en/faife/professional-codes-of-ethics-for-librarians (accessed Aug. 30, 2010).
5. Larry Nucci, "Culture, Context, and the Psychological Sources of Human Rights Concepts," in *Morality in Context*, ed. Wolfgang Edelstein and Gertrud Nunner-Winkler, Advances in Psychology, vol. 137 (Amsterdam, The Netherlands: Elsevier, 2005), 371.
6. Ibid., 368.
7. Ibid., 367.
8. Henning Mankell, remarks delivered at Gothenburg, Sweden, annual IFLA conference: August 11, 2010, at the University of Gothenburg Library.
9. Helen Nissenbaum, *Privacy in Context: Technology, Policy, and the Integrity of Social Life* (Stanford, CA: Stanford University Press, 2009).

Chapter 3

User-Generated Content

Eli Neiburger

Abstract

The emergence of Web 2.0, with its emphasis on user-generated content, has tremendous potential for library marketing, services, and community building. However, the open nature of these communications and the ambiguous nature of authorship creates major privacy and security challenges. This chapter of Privacy and Freedom of Information in 21st-Century Libraries *examines those issues in depth, and provides best practices for addressing some uncertainties.*

So, here we are in the twenty-first century! Isn't it great? We've got picturephones in our pockets, dancing bipedal robots, high-definition digital television, international space stations, large hadron colliders, and even an electric car or two. No jetpacks yet, but I hear they're coming. And we've got this thing called Web 2.0, which supposedly unites all human knowledge and creativity into one vast hyperlinked knowledge space or something, right? I read about it on Wikipedia when I was looking for details about Yoda's mom.

Web 2.0 is the buzzword to rule them all. It's such a powerful idea that it quickly infected nearby institutions, giving us Business 2.0, Health 2.0, Government 2.0, and yes, Library 2.0. While each of these permutations is generally used to support whatever argument the user wanted to make in the first place, there was a significant change that came with the Web 2.0 upgrade, one that is deeply disruptive to libraries. While Web 1.0 was all about broadcast and publishing, replacing brochures, phone books, catalogs, and travel agents, Web 2.0 turned the channel upside down with the realization that content flowing up from the users is just as (if not more) valuable than the content flowing outward from the content producers.

This is a pretty big shakeup for institutions that built their value proposition on some sort of unimpeachable, impartial notion of content authority, and it can be a bitter pill to swallow for management cultures that still aren't certain if this whole Internet thing is really worth it. When you add to this well-ensconced reluctance a hearty dollop of legal murkiness and a pinch of terrifying worst-case scenarios, and stir with distant or disinterested campus or municipal legal counsel, that's a recipe for a steaming hot bowl of "We'll just stay here in the twentieth century where things make SENSE" stew. Just like Grandma used to make.

The major challenge for libraries and library staff that want to ride the Web 2.0 wave and start benefiting from user-generated content is that there is a heap of very good and very unanswered questions swirling around the edges of privacy and freedom of information on library Web presences when you let the patrons in on the act. If a patron contributes a review of a book to your site, who owns it? Who owns it if it's an awesome review you might want to use in a print ad? Who owns it if it's horrible and racist and you've got to do something about it? Who owns it if the FBI would like to know more about who posted it? Who owns it if it was actually originally written by some big shot with a small army of besuited lawyers and they want you to take it down? Who owns it if the poster has gotten death threats about what she wrote in her review and she wants you to take it down?

Most importantly, just how freaked out should libraries really be about this issue? And, if they want to answer some of these questions, where on earth do they start? While fully acknowledging that I am not remotely an attorney, I'm certainly not your attorney, and in no way is any of the following to be construed as legal advice, and that these words bear no warranties, either expressed or implied, I'd like to offer up some best- and worst-case scenarios surrounding user-generated content and twenty-first-century libraries from the perspective of a library administrator who deals with this stuff every day and hopefully give you some tools with which to soothe the flustered and encourage the timid.

Ownership and Copyright

Considering that most of the Copyright Act would expressly forbid many of the things that happen in libraries every day if it weren't for our old friends first sale and fair use, library staff sure do worry a lot about protecting the rights of the copyright holder at the expense of the patron. This mindset makes sense defensively for the organization's interests, but the tendency is often to err on the side of caution, which can turn library staff into overzealous copyright enforcers a little too much like the police who try to stop tourists from photographing public art because they might violate the artists' copyright.

The question of ownership is actually relatively straightforward. According to the Copyright Act of 1978, as soon as a creator commits a creation to some tangible medium, he automatically and instantly holds the copyright for that content. While there's certainly some gray area, posting something to a website involves some actual flipping of microscopic bits of metal from pointing one way to pointing another way on some hard disk somewhere, so in practice, as soon as someone posts something to your site, he owns it. Now, there are ways for this to not be so, such as setting up terms of use or some other agreement that the user does not read but agrees to anyway that says that the library holds the copyright on anything contributed to the site, but in general, it's not a good idea to claim copyright on the contributions of your users for several reasons.

First, as we're about to explore, the worst-case scenarios here definitely play out better if the library does not hold the copyright and is not directly responsible for the contributions of the users. Most of the nightmares work out better this way. There is also a simple legal mechanism that allows the library to ensure that it is not responsible for some of the contributions of users (registering as a service provider) that we'll get to later, but the bigger issue is that libraries, as fundamental and beloved underminers of copyright through our positively socialist circulating collections, should be working to encourage and spread free and fair use, not investing in tools, techniques, and billable hours that aim to restrict the use of their Web content.

Like most of the difficult questions facing libraries in this century, it comes down to a question about the value proposition that libraries offer to their users and what models of content distribution we wish to adopt. News organizations and other periodical publishers hold tight to their copyright and need to police the use of their material to ensure that nobody's getting a free ride. This clearly is not a model that libraries should emulate: first, as you may have noticed, those industries are not transitioning to the twenty-first century all that well; and second, the value of libraries to their user communities is in access to information, not in their ability to derive income from copyrights they may hold.

A better model for libraries that want to welcome the contributions of their users is something that many libraries already have: an open bulletin board where users can post what they like and the library will tend to it as appropriate. Taking that service online doesn't really change much, but the fact that it's open to the world can make the time-honored seem foreboding and threatening.

Worst-Case Scenarios

So what's the worst that could happen, and how might a library respond if it does happen? It's worth mentioning that each of these are quite edgy edge cases, and while they certainly don't represent the realities of day-to-day management of user-contributed content, these are the types of questions that typically get fretted about when a library is considering opening its site to user contribution, and having answers to these questions up front can save many hours of meetings and probably even avoid the formations of otherwise unnecessary committees.

"You stole my book review!"

Let's give this complainer the benefit of the doubt and assume that this is demonstrably true. The content that a user submitted to your site appeared earlier elsewhere attributed to someone else, and someone claiming to be this someone else found the content on your site and wants you to take it down. She may be wealthy and well-armed with attorneys on retainer, or she may be just another one of those patrons who says this kind of thing every chance they get.

In this situation, the safe course of action is simply to take down the offending content. Whoever posted it apparently didn't hold the copyright to that content, and if the publishing on your site is not permitted by the copyright holder, it's infringing. While there are certainly defenses that could allow you to keep the content up, such as fair use or focusing on the fact that the contributions belong to the contributors and Ms. Stole-My-Review should take it up with them, unless the contributed content is of extremely high value or the claim of infringement is highly dubious, just taking it down is the simple solution to this scenario.

Note that if you registered as a service provider as described below, it's unlikely that you would be liable for any damages as a result of your infringement, but that, as always, doesn't mean that Ms. Stole-My-Review can't sue you for damages, which can be just as expensive. See the section Exposure and Risk below.

"That's defamatory; take it down!"

While it may seem that this is a no-brainer, there can be a lot more uncertainty surrounding the claim itself in this circumstance. For example, if a user tagged all of a particular author's books as "Written by a racist [expletive]," that can be relatively cut-and-dried. But if someone writes in a review that "All this guy's books STINK," is that defamation? And what if all those books really do stink? Does that matter?

Published defamation, or libel, is serious business, but it is also a favorite battle cry of the disturbed or deluded. Avoiding liability for torts such as libel is another good reason to make it clear that the comments are the opinions of the poster, not the institution, but in many circumstances it's again wise to make some kind of response to claims like this as a show of good faith, which is important if Mr. My-Books-Do-Not-All-Stink drags you to court.

Sometimes it may be enough for the library to exercise a little editorial control when these issues come up, as it may be a particular word that's getting the complainant so fired up. Maybe he doesn't mind being called a racist, it's the expletive that bothers him. Or you could change the review to "All this guy's books [are not good in my opinion]." However, if the complainant is mad enough, this won't likely help. One thing to note whenever the library exercises editorial control is that it's important to always do so transparently to retain the trust of your users. This means make it clear that the content has been edited and why, such as appending "[edited for publication]" to the end of the review or otherwise calling out the edits. And really, is that "racist [expletive]" tag really adding any value anyway? It's certainly a reasonable response to just delete the content at issue.

However, depending on how strongly you feel about the content that's being complained about, and whether you've registered as a service provider, and how much risk your organization is willing to bear to defend the statement that all the guy's books really do stink, you can certainly just say, "Your books do stink, and we're not taking it down. Go away." But if it ever gets to trial, you can safely assume that the judge, or the jury, wouldn't consider that a show of good faith.

"The library director is a stupid [expletive], and don't you dare restrict my speech!"

What about when the users are contributing horrible, villainous, defamatory statements about the library, its staff, or its leaders? You'd better believe this one is no edge case; it happens all the time. So how is this different from libel about authors or other posters? Legally, it's not very different, but how you handle it will be far more visible to your patrons than pulling a rude tag from an inferior item would be.

It's worth considering how poorly many organizations, especially municipal bodies, typically handle public criticism online, so this is a big opportunity to differentiate the library by handling foaming vitriol with grace and aplomb. If you err on the side of letting as many comments stand as possible, editing out only the words that are really over the line with asterisks or a well-placed [ahem], always making note that the content has been edited, the library can really only gain by demonstrating its commitment to free speech and tolerance of criticism. You might even win back the black hearts of the foul-mouthed patrons who want the card catalog back or make similarly unreasonable requests.

One other aspect to consider here when trapped in a thought experiment on this issue is that often, you can count on other users of the site to rebuke the vitriol or at least disagree with it. Honest, unprovoked disagreement and defense of the library from other patrons is priceless and will turn more minds in a positive direction than could ever be negatively influenced by a diatribe.

Finally, as they always do, the critics claiming that you're violating the First Amendment if you so much as touch their filth-ridden masterpiece have a bit of a point. The library is supposed to be a haven for First Amendment expression, and it would be an attractive, high-profile case for free speech advocates if the library is caught censoring its own criticism. There's no upside to suppressing library criticism, and it is indeed on shaky political ground. Whatever PR hit the missive might initially bring can be readily canceled and even inverted by calm, cool, permissive moderation of the thread and response to the concerns, no matter how malicious, cruel, or plainly insane they might be.

Best-Case Scenarios

Although the preceding worst cases can be pretty scary, especially when budgets are tight and legal defense funds are scarce, it's always important to have some best-case scenarios in mind to help staff and management understand the possibilities and potential of user-contributed content and what they might miss out on if they're unwilling the bear the rather remote risk of a worst case. "Because it's cool and Amazon is doing it" is not a solid foundation for a library service; here are some scenarios around ownership and copyright that show the positives of user-contributed content.

"Hey! That's my grandpa! Here's his diary!"

While we always worry that we'll hear "Hey! That's my grandpa! TAKE IT DOWN!" it's much more likely that allowing user-generated content will lead to more contributions, more engaged users, and better information for the library to share, especially if you're not encumbering any donated content or information with onerous license agreements or regressive copyright stances. When the Brooklyn Museum started posting its photos of the Columbian Exposition on Flickr, it quickly discovered a commenter in Seattle who was making detailed, carefully researched notes on the images and adding value to the collection far beyond the efforts of staff or local volunteers (www.flickr.com/photos/brooklyn_museum/2784217831/; see comments and tags by Rob Ketcherside).

Allowing users to post and still own their images, reviews, comments, or other content positions the library right where it's always been—as the place where a community stores its critical information. It's of high value to the community to have a trusted, permanent place to put this stuff, and while it seems right now as though commercial Web services such as Flickr are the solution to this problem, once Yahoo inevitably gives Flickr the Geocities treatment (shutting it down unceremoniously and rebuffing all attempts to preserve its content), people won't feel the same way about freely giving their precious content to corporations. Libraries are well-positioned to develop services that compete with these commercial services, provided that we outperform them on use rights, organization, and local focus. If you paint the user's rights into a corner with overly restrictive or regressive terms of use or license agreements, the library won't seem as useful in comparison to our online archival rivals.

"Here is a review of every new mystery you buy."

If our most passionate users feel that the library is a safe, fair place to contribute their opinions, ratings, and reviews, a place that doesn't assert the same ownership of their speech that Amazon or Facebook does, their obsessions can lead them to provide value to the library that the library would never otherwise obtain. Allowing patrons to feel good about contributing content to the library without feeling like they're getting fleeced and resold behind the scenes can develop the library as the prime receptacle of their critical output. Completism is also a powerful force and one that libraries can harness over time by allowing the contributors to see the fruits of their labor; by telling them what percentage of a collection they've reviewed or how many patrons have requested an item after reading their review. Reviews are everywhere, but when a library collects reviews from its own community of users, many users will prize those opinions beyond anything from *Kirkus* or *PW*. Develop contributor-friendly, human-readable use policies, and your friendly neighborhood contributors will feel good about contributing.

"I've tagged every book with a vampire in it with 'Vampire.'"

Tagging isn't really the ownership or copyright hotbed that reviews or contributed photos might be, but it's still worth remembering how much value your patrons can add to your discovery tools if you'd just let them. And trust them. While few patrons worry about who owns their tags, if they don't show up immediately because they need to go through some approval queue, the patrons get the message immediately: you don't trust them. While we certainly know that we have some good reasons not to trust them, the reality is that the risk of really dangerous tags appearing is very low, tags are easy to clean up, and the negative impression given by a tag-approval queue is much greater than someone actually seeing an objectionable tag applied insouciantly. As you're considering the legal issues associated with user-contributed content, remember that an approval queue cannot protect you completely from a lawsuit, but it can ensure that your tagging project fails by constantly reminding your best contributors how little you trust them. Trust them and harness the power of their obsessions!

Responsibility and Privacy

It can be depressing how lackadaisical these whippersnappers are about their privacy. We're trying to protect their right to read freely, and there they go blabbing to all of Facebook that they just checked out *Living with Bursitis*. It's tempting to view our position as old school and pointless, but this pendulum is likely to swing back in the 10s, and one of the biggest advantages we have as libraries is that we still care fiercely about privacy and that our users widely feel that their personal data is safe at the library.

This gets a little more complex when the users start contributing intentionally public information to the library's Web presence. Are we compromising a user's checkout history by allowing anyone on the Web to see what items that person has reviewed? Are users fully aware of how the data that the library has about them is connected and available? We don't want patrons' library experiences to remind them of Facebook, where you know that you're exposed but not sure where or how to address it. Also, when accepting public contributions from a user, what information should and could the library store about the contributor, and what do we have to tell to who if they come asking?

Library data has certainly been a political football in this century, and it's likely that there's a turnover somewhere in the future. But, as Spiderman is always sort of saying, with great power comes great responsibility, and with sloppy grandstanding legislation comes opportunity. In all the PATRIOT Act hubbub, there was little attention paid to the fact that there were no requirements for what data libraries kept or how long they kept it. When you're talking about checkouts, there's certain data that we've always needed to keep to ensure that we could either get our stuff back or at least unleash the collection agencies, but with Web contributions, you don't generally need that stuff. This means that you don't need to require a library card number, name, or address before someone can contribute comments, tags, reviews, or photos to the library's website; what you collect is up to you. Although most patrons will choose to just use the account that's already connected to their library card number, you can bet that the cagey or paranoid ones will figure out that they can have two accounts, one to track their card use and another for contributing. It doesn't make sense to require this of patrons, but having it as an option is an excellent, straightforward way for contributors to remain private.

As far as what you should collect, it's always a good idea to collect the IP address from which a contribution came, as it can help the library to diagnose problems or track down abuse, but that isn't necessarily personally identifying information (in fact, it rarely is these days), and if you want to err on the side of maximum privacy, you could remove the IP addresses after some period of time has elapsed, say twenty-four hours or a week or a month. Other than IP address and e-mail, what more do you need to allow someone to contribute to your website? Generally, you ought to know if contributors are human or not to keep out spam, but who knows? Maybe a future law will make this kind of discrimination against digital citizens illegal.

In any case, if someone contributes something threatening, scary, or ominous to your website, and law enforcement—local, state, or federal—comes asking about it, what do you do? This is actually no scarier or newer than the situation that every library is already in, if you consider that a patron contributes checkout data to the library when they check something out. Every library should know what it plans to do when law enforcement asks for data that it holds (Call the director!), and it's no different whether they're asking about checkout history or details of a questionable post on the website. At least, it shouldn't be any different. Patron data is patron data, and information about user contributions is no more and no less important and private than checkout history.

Worst-Case Scenarios

It's easy to think that a G-man asking about posting history, or even seizing your servers because he doesn't like your answer, is a worst-case scenario. And it's pretty horrifying. But it's not as bad as keeping too much data, having lax security, and having all your patron data silently lifted from your server without anyone knowing until patrons' credit reports start going sour . . . but that's more of an IT issue than a policy issue. Let's stick with the policy issues for now:

"Hello, I'm Agent Smith. Who posted this comment?"

As I said above, a solid response to this is "Let me get you in touch with the director." But the situation you want to avoid from a policy perspective is "We know, but we're not going to tell you." That can lead to a court order to seize your servers instead of a court order for you to release the data. Your library should have a policy, procedure, or understanding about what to do when law enforcement shows up with questions, and the source of the data shouldn't matter. If people worry that allowing user-contributed content would increase the likelihood of this scenario, well, so does running a library. The only way to avoid this risk is to close up!

"Hello, I'm Google. I already know who tagged this."

The real front on privacy at the library is the data that we don't control, and many systems that facilitate user-contributed content keep the data on company servers far outside your library's sphere of policy influence. Agent Smith doesn't even need to harangue the folks at the circ desk if he can just go right to Google or your vendor or some other party that doesn't have a library's commitment to privacy but has the information he needs. If you host your library blog on Blogspot or WordPress.org or TypePad or anywhere other than your own servers, the fact is that you're not in control of access to that data, no matter what the vendor says. And remember that any page you add Google Analytics code to will have the details of every subsequent access stored on a server somewhere under Google's control. Although there may not have been problems yet, that's generally because the boundaries haven't yet been pushed. There are lots of good reasons to keep Web services in house, but control over privacy and access is by far the best reason to keep this data close.

"Hello, I'm Nutty Patron. Why did you tell Agent Smith I posted that secret comment?"

It's always a challenge to handle paranoid delusional patrons. It's even harder when they know a bit about what they're talking about and you can't really reassure them that their personal data is safe. Having a board-approved privacy policy that covers what is kept and under what circumstances it can be divulged is a good idea, although it can arouse more suspicion than it dispels if it's too specific about circumstances of release. Maintaining the trust of the community is critical for twenty-first-century libraries, and that starts with transparent and sustainable privacy policies.

Best Case Scenarios

Done carefully and thoughtfully, a library's position on the privacy of its patrons can set a community standard for how such things should be handled, and the privacy of their interactions with the library can be an important part of the library's value proposition.

"I'm contributing this to the library because I know they'll keep my identity safe."

Although few patrons yet look at things so defensively, libraries again have an opportunity to differentiate themselves from other community organizations by being upfront, straightforward, and progressive about the privacy of its patrons, as we've always been. As users begin to contribute publicly to the library, ensure that they are in control of what is exposed and what is protected, and always make new services opt-in. One of the challenges of the library is that for every patron who desperately wants to keep data secret, there's another patron who would very much like to share that data with friends or the world. Don't pull a Facebook; make the privacy controls and policies simple and err on the side of privacy, and the public will trust that their contributions to the library are in good hands.

"I'm a bit nutty, so I won't tag things at the library so Agent Smith can't find me."

The flip side of allowing people to opt in to use the services they want and expose the data they want to expose is that when you make it clear what opting in means, the more paranoid patrons can just not opt in or use those services and keep their account as private as possible. This seems straightforward, but getting it right can be tricky when you're making design decisions from a position of fully understanding all the library's services and options. It's a good idea to make it as clear as possible; for example, putting "Turning this on will expose your username and any reviews you submit to the Web. You can always turn it off later from this page" right under the button to opt in is a good idea. On the gripping hand, you don't want to be one of those libraries that have contradictory, overly wordy signage everywhere, even on their website, and you want to make sure that the user experience of your website doesn't become a barrage of warnings. Like anything else at a library, it's about finding a balance between the right amount of information for the casual user and for the concerned user.

"Users who commented on this also commented on this."

When you've earned the trust of your users, you can roll out new features that anonymously leverage the data you've collected to provide high-value new services without your users immediately assuming you're up to no good. For example, it's possible, without compromising the privacy of the involved users, to compare the checkout histories of multiple users to show users that other people who checked out an item also checked out another item. If users always opt in for services more on the edge of privacy issues, and if you make it clear what they're signing up for, there are opportunities to get some really great data and develop helpful services without the patrons feeling like they're being used. Again, this depends on a policy framework that includes a privacy policy, opt-in procedures, and terms of use that are readable and accessible to users; no easy task!

Exposure and Risk

Navigating the twenty-first century is no easy task for libraries. It's difficult to know what to do next, what's most important, where the risk to the organization is acceptable, and where it's unacceptable. Part of assessing the risk of a new idea is assessing the legal exposure that is related to the idea, but too often, the line between exposure and risk is blurred to the point where any exposure is considered risk. It's true that exposure can be risky, but simply put, not all legal exposure is risk, and when the place of libraries in our society is as tenuous as it is at this moment, it's critical to understand the difference between exposure and risk when determining what to do next. A big part of the responsibility for making this distinction is borne by your legal counsel. A good attorney will be able to tell you with a reasonable degree of certainty where the legal exposure is for your organization as you consider services that include user-contributed content. A great attorney will also give you an opinion on what degree of risk is associated with that exposure. While we don't all get to choose our counsel, especially on campuses or as a part of a county or other parent entity, sometimes just asking separately about the exposure and the risk associated with a new idea can help illuminate the way forward.

For example, consider the earlier scenario of the

plagiarized review. If you distributed an infringing review via your website, even for a minute, and even if you took it down, there can technically be exposure and potential for a damage award. However, there is very little risk of an actual suit, because even if the complainant is fully lawyered up, the lawyers will likely start with a cease-and-desist letter, and if you honor it, the matter is likely closed. So when you allow users to post reviews, there is conceivably some exposure if a user posts infringing content. But there may be very little risk of a suit, a trial, and an award if you are responsive to complaints.

The flip side of this is that the lawyers may not send a cease-and-desist letter; they may just sue. However, anybody can sue your library over anything for any reason. It's not hard. This turns around the risk calculus when you consider that quite simply, there is not a single solitary thing that a library can do for which it is safe from litigation. Because litigation is expensive on any scale, through this lens there is risk everywhere, in every single action.

The other complicating factor is that many of the issues surrounding user-contributed content haven't had their landmark cases yet. They haven't been tried, so no one really knows with complete certainty where the exposure is and where it isn't. There are some hot spots, sure, but only twentieth-century libraries can avoid these issues completely. And even they can get sued, whenever, for anything!

So when developing new services, or when you're just trying to get your library to do what many other libraries are already doing, it's important to assess both the exposure of the new service and the risk of the new service to be sure that the two aren't being conflated into one big fat NO. In addition, it's worth remembering that there are ways to limit the library's exposure, such as the service provider registration or terms of use that require the contributor to indemnify the library against litigation and damages. Those methods can shield the library's assets from predatory litigation and decrease the financial exposure, but the risk of facing a suit isn't really any different, and the PR cost of a suit that breaks the wrong way, even if it's not costing the library money, can be huge.

So, while remembering my disclaimers about my non-attorneyness and this not being legal advice, when you're working to build consensus around a new service that is perceived as legally risky, try separating the exposure and then planning responses to potential complaints that would mitigate the risk of damages or a case going to trial. Think, "If we get a C&D, we'll just take it down," or "We'll make a good faith effort to determine the ownership of the image if it is in question," as such approaches can make a big difference if things ever get ugly.

Also, don't forget, the chance of things ever getting ugly like this is really pretty low in the first place. Libraries aren't often perceived as having deep pockets, and fair use casts a wide net of protection over a library's use of copyrighted material that makes pursuing infringement by a library a pretty long shot with a fairly poisonous PR landscape; suing a library is fortunately still not a very popular thing to do.

Worst-Case Scenarios

Let's hope you never have to face these, but the reality is that the risk of litigation is simply part of doing business as a library, and a lawsuit, even one that goes to trial, is not the end of the world, although you'll probably wish it were.

"I'm suing you because you published this awful comment."

Nasty things will eventually get said in any online forum. How you handle this situation will impact both the exposure and the risk of accepting user-contributed content; something as simple as a Report This Post button can make it clear to users, attorneys, and judges that there is a mechanism for dealing with content that is undesirable. It's also standard for complaints to begin with an actual complaint or cease-and-desist letter; that will give you a chance to respond to the complaint by taking down or editing the post before a suit is filed. Complainants who don't first give you a chance to resolve the issue before filing suit aren't acting in very good faith, but that doesn't mean they can't file a suit. But the judge probably won't like it too much.

The other way to handle this risk is to monitor or moderate contributions more proactively, but considering the low level of risk associated with someone talking trash on the library's website, it's unlikely that heavy monitoring would be worth the hassle, expense, or distrustful message that it sends to users. The bottom line is that this can happen, but it's unlikely, and if it does, you'll probably get a chance to fix it before things get out of hand. That should be a reasonable risk considering the potential value that your users can contribute to the site.

"I'm suing you because you infringed my copyright."

Again, this one is fairly unlikely (What kind of a loser goes around stealing Kirkus reviews and passing them off as her own on library websites?) and is likely subject to all the same opportunities to resolve as the above, with one additional bonus: fair use. Fair use is not protection against a claim of infringement against a library, but it is very effective protection against a judgment of infringement by a library, and therefore a powerful deterrent against suing a library for copyright infringement. But again, we don't want to do this on purpose, so if it comes to your attention, plan to resolve it and move on. If it's so rewarding to post on your website that users are actually plagiarizing to get content worthy to post, then you are doing great!

"I'm suing you because you compromised my online identity."

Okay, this is a scary one. Don't do it! There's a much stronger argument here that the damage is done once it's done and that no cease-and-desist response can remediate it, and this is a very gray area, so it's hard to know what will happen. Fortunately, the types who are throwing up unlikely risky scenarios in an attempt to make your project go away probably won't think of this one. However, it's another good reason to have a solid privacy policy, your data under your control, and strong security to make sure this doesn't happen. On the flip side, in most cases it will be difficult to establish damages, which again won't protect you from a suit being filed, but will probably limit the risk of what is already a very unlikely occurrence.

Best-Case Scenarios

If you're already involved in litigation, it may seem like there is no best-case scenario as the billable hours mount up. But if you had your ducks in a row in the first place, responded to early complaints, and have a policy backing up your actions, the risk of a big loss can be pretty low. Another way of looking at these situations is that your case might wind up establishing a precedent that makes further pursuit of similar claims much less likely. So get out there and take one for the team!

"Case dismissed!"

There are a lot of reasons for a case not to reach trial. If you've registered as a service provider, your liability for copyright infringement claims is limited, and that can be enough. If you acted in good faith or the plaintiff failed to act in good faith, that can be enough. But if it gets this far, you want to have had the policy established in advance, have acted in good faith, and have the attorneys with the knowledge and skills to make it go away as soon as possible.

"I won't take your case because you have no case and no money."

If someone really wants to sue your library over some user-contributed content, he's going to. But if he is going to get a skilled attorney to help him, he'll probably need either a case or some money. Because the likelihood of bad things happening on your library website is relatively low, and you've got the policy and the good faith (right?), someone who is just angry may have a hard time finding someone who thinks he has a case. Of course, if he has deep pockets, or even just pockets, it may not matter if he has a case or not; he can get his fancy attorney uncle to file papers for him, and the law allows anyone to sue anyone for anything!

"Are you insane? You want to sue a library?"

Of course it happens, but nobody likes to see libraries get beat up! Random angry and offensive Internet posters might not care about this, but if you're worried about unintentionally crossing some Gigantic Megacorp Inc. and having its expensively suited in-house counsel serve papers on you without so much as a letter telling you what the problem is first, well, the risk of that happening is very low. Libraries are less threatening to corporations than ever, and even if the legal department says they have a case, the PR department will likely say, "Are you insane?"

Licenses and Terms of Use

As the twenty-first century continues to unfold, libraries are thinking a lot about copyright and fair use and first sale and all that stuff, but the real action, and the real threats to the status quo, lie in binding language that is not contained in the copyright code at all: the license agreements that are attached to e-books or software and the terms of use that are ignored by website users of all levels of paranoia. For example, there are libraries that are circulating Kindles loaded with books. It's pretty clear that the Kindle terms of use don't allow that sort of thing, but that makes it actionable, not illegal. So will Amazon pursue this? Most likely not while only a handful of libraries are doing it, but if the practice spreads, who knows? The courts have found that "clickwrap" licenses, like the ones everybody clicks right past several times a day on the Web, are binding and enforceable, and do you know how many of those your library has agreed to, or that your patrons are agreeing to, right this very moment? Me neither, but I bet if you tried to make a conservative estimate of the potential legal liability being taken on each day at a busy library, you would run screaming to yank the Internet plug right out of the wall.

So, there are two ways of looking at this complexity and risk that our organizations tolerate each day. One is to set all the risk of doing new things as the cost of doing business, dwarfed by the complexity of still-cooking Web law, and that if you're going to not do things because there is some risk and uncertainty involved, well, you won't be doing anything anytime ever. The other approach is to use these dark instruments to become part of the legal background radiation of twenty-first-century life and have some more substantial legal infrastructure behind the library's exposures to help everybody involved be a little more comfortable with scary things like blog comments and online photos. The one caution here, as before, is to be aware that special place that libraries hold in many patrons' hearts and to step outside that place only with very solid reason; many people see clickthrough End User License Agreements (EULAs) as just another way that the corporations will getcha and one that we are all powerless to resist or change, but that doesn't mean that they'll tolerate their library behaving that way.

How and Why to Register as an Online Service Provider

While the legal powers of the twenty-first century can appear to be forming up on the other side of the battle lines from a library's perspective, every once in a while we can find ourselves on the side of some major players, and their ability to get what they want out of government can rub off on us a bit. An excellent example of this is the provision in the 1998 Digital Millennium Copyright Act (DMCA) that limits an online service provider's liability for copyright infringement by its users if it has designated an agent to handle any claims that might arise. While the law predates YouTube, YouTube is the best example of why this mechanism was put in place; if YouTube was on the hook for infringing content that people uploaded to YouTube, well, there would be no YouTube.

Because an online service provider is defined as a provider of online services (tautology much?) and libraries provide online services, this means that a library can fill out the shockingly straightforward Interim Designation of Agent to Receive Notification of Claimed Infringement form, pay $105, and designate itself as its own agent to handle copyright claims arising from content posted by users to the websites it operates. In return, the registered online service provider's liability for copyright infringement by its users is significantly limited. Not eliminated, but it's a safe bet that it's more than $105 worth of liability that will be limited.

U.S. Copyright Office Online Service Provider Registration
www.copyright.gov/onlinesp/

Note that this does not shield the library from other damages that could be pursued as a result of user contributions; you're still on the hook for libel or other torts, but when you consider that copyright infringement is a big piece of the liability out there on the Web, this simple action can put a lot of comfort and surety behind a new initiative.

Forcing Release under Specific Licenses, Progressive or Regressive

In addition to the service provider's protection from copyright infringement claims, your library's Web products can have binding terms of use posted at the bottom of every page, where users can safely ignore them, or on the user registration form, where users can obliviously click past them, or on the Content Submit page, where users will check whatever checkboxes you tell them to. These terms of use can be used essentially to get the user to agree to whatever you want or need for people involved to feel that the risk has been mitigated. For example, your terms of use could specify that by contributing content to this website, the user agrees to defend and indemnify the library against any and all claims arising from the content they post, including payment of any attorneys' fees that may be required. Who would agree to that, right? Bought anything from iTunes lately?

Or, your terms of use could specify that anything a user contributes to the site permanently becomes the sole property of the library, its heirs and assigns, and so on. Who would agree to that? It's crazy! Posted anything to Facebook or Twitter lately?

Or your terms of use could specify that anything a user contributes to the site will be released to the Web under a Creative Commons Noncommercial Attribution license, meaning that anyone anywhere will be able to reuse that content, with attribution, for any noncommercial purpose, without specific permission. Sounds great, right? Except that noncommercial doesn't necessarily mean nice, respectful, or positive. Downloading a photo of Grandpa and adding a Hitler mustache and reuploading it is completely noncommercial and is easily attributed, and now you can't even use a trumped-up copyright infringement claim to take it down.

Again, with great power comes great responsibility. Terms of use are a tried-and-true way of binding the actions of your users to certain conditions. You just need to decide what those conditions are. You could claim ownership of everything they post to make sure that your investment in obtaining it cannot be easily eroded. You could make sure that the library is not on the financial hook in most legal situations (but don't forget that anyone can be sued by anyone for anything), or you could strike another of those tricky balances between protecting the interests of the library and helping patrons to see a model of progressive, patron-oriented use rights that have a reason for existence beyond protecting the library.

Worst-Case Scenarios

It used to be that unless you were a professional content creator, you had relatively little day-to-day interaction with copyright in any form. But here in the twenty-first century, everybody brushes up against copyright law and practice multiple times per day with unpredictable consequences. In addition, now that anyone can be a professional content creator (no sniggering please), you've got people who believe that they should be paid anytime someone looks at something they wrote, but who are also completely comfortable helping themselves to professionally produced movies or music for free. It's a recipe for some angry library patrons, such as the following situations:

"I have to read all this legal crap just to tag an item? Forget it!"

Just because people click through countless EULAs every day doesn't mean they like it when their library hits them with one. We all know libraries are often held to a different standard, for good or ill, and it's much more likely that patrons would throw up their hands when confronted with an unreadable EULA when trying to register or contribute at the library, especially because few libraries would be likely to play the usability tricks with EULAs that corporate websites do all the time, like a login button labeled "I agree to these terms" or other perfectly legal but not very user-oriented obfuscations.

It's an unfortunate fact that patrons often expect a certain amount of rigmarole from the library in order to gain access. It's the Ghost of Librarianship Past, and unfortunately Present and even Future, and it's got decades of life left in it. That's why you should carefully consider how, when, and where your terms of use are presented to the user to make sure that you strike a balance between informed consent and the Web user's tendency to find the minimum allowable number of clicks to get what they want.

"I don't want to upload my video if you won't protect it."

In this age of transition, there are a lot of conflicting ideas out there about how content should behave on the Web. One generation is big into information that wants to be free, while their parents and grandparents would still prefer that nobody steals from them, especially information. This makes for a unique tension between the desire to share and the desire to control. You may have patrons who are happy to share their video if you can promise them than nobody will ever do anything inappropriate with it. That's not a promise you can realistically make with content on the open Web, even if you wanted to, and you don't want to. Sometimes just the act of reading through comprehensive terms of use can put highly unlikely nightmare scenarios into heads that never would have thought of those things otherwise, leading to anxiety and a fight-or-flight response, and really, you don't want your patrons having to decide whether they should fight your terms of use or run from them. If you hit them with the legalese at the wrong time, in the wrong way, like every time they go to upload something, you increase the risk of their souring on the whole endeavor or drive them to harangue your staff or board in pursuit of impossible promises (like nothing bad will ever happen) before they'll give you content that you'd really like to have!

"My brother went to law school, and he says I shouldn't sign this."

The last thing you want to do is prompt scrutiny of your terms of use in a way that leads your patrons to finally realize the kinds of crazy things they've been agreeing to when they agree to those things. Boilerplate can be ominously unintelligible at best and horrifically out-to-get-you at worst. It's likely that many of your patrons would be shocked by some of the things your attorney expects them to agree to if the things were clearly explained. With overly broad or overly unreadable terms of use, you run the risk of someone trying to puzzle them out to disastrous effect. Again, a balance between ironclad contract language and something more like an executive summary of what the contributor is agreeing to is needed to prevent your project from missing out on some great contributions just because the contributor has access to questionable free legal advice.

Best-Case Scenarios

So given all those ways your implementation of terms of use can go wrong, and combined with the ever-present fact that bears repeating that anybody can sue anybody for anything, what's the case for solid terms of use? What's there for the library to gain if anybody actually agrees to them? Of course they're going to agree to them; it's just another legally binding checkbox, right?

"What do you mean, I don't have to ask to use this?"

With the best of intentions, libraries have managed to reinforce the rights of the copyright holders over and over and over again at the expense of the user's rights under fair use or otherwise; this has helped to create a expectation that something on the Web, even on the website of a public library, is ferociously defended and if you plan to use it in any way, you'd better have express written permission. If you put your terms of use together right, you can reset both the contributor's expectations and the consumer's use rights to the mutual benefit of all involved. This means that you could put on your image gallery webpages, instead of a list of prohibited uses, a list of allowed uses that includes most of the things people usually want to do with things they get at the library. For example, there are many reasons that kids doing a report can legitimately use an image from the Web, and yet all kinds of otherwise respectable grownups tell the kids they'd better get an answer from someone at the Smithsonian before they impact the commercial potential of that photo of a old bicycle by using it in their eighth grade term paper. The library's approach to use rights can be a key differentiator between the library's Web presence and commercial alternatives; don't miss the opportunity to make this clear with uniform, permissive noncommercial use rights for content your users contribute, backed up by your terms of use!

"Case dismissed; the terms of use that you agreed to clearly state . . ."

The strongest reason to do this and do it right is because it can really save you if the library does find itself heading to court over a user contribution. If it says in your terms of use that by using your site, the user agrees that all content contributed by users of the site is the property and opinion of the contributor and in no way represents the views of your organization, its staff, board, regents, mascots, heirs and assigns, and so on, the guy who wants to sue the library because the library said in a patron review that his book stinks has much less of a case. Again, that doesn't mean he can't sue you. It just makes it less likely that he'll win, which means it's less likely to happen.

Similarly, if someone decides to sue the library because something she uploaded to the library was later misused by someone else, your terms of use could make it clear that the library is not responsible for that or even require that the submitter waive the right to sue over something like that. Again, that does not mean that she can't sue you for it. It just means it won't get very far if you can produce evidence that she agreed to a covenant not to sue you over it.

"Wow, the library has all this great stuff in the Creative Commons!"

The reality (call it fortunate or unfortunate, depending on your perspective on such things) is that our twenty-first-century audiences are getting a lot more sophisticated about this kind of stuff. While this may mean that they have some unrealistic ideas here and there, it also means that the notion of the public domain or other bodies of content that are free and easy to use is a popular idea that's growing by leaps and bounds. This is a clear opportunity for the library to position itself in opposition to the draconian use rights of most commercial content and be a part of the Open Web.

Creative Commons is a big, great idea that's been wholeheartedly embraced by the growing, influential Creative Class, and as more teachers, librarians, and creators are becoming comfortable with it and all the things you don't have to worry about when you use Creative Commons licenses, it's growing into a body of content that is as free and easy to use as we wished everything was. What better value proposition for a library to offer to its twenty-first-century users than a bunch of stuff, by and about their own community, that is free for them to use in most ways? It's really what we've been doing for decades, taking things and making them easier to access. In creating your terms of use, you have a chance to position the library as leading the way towards a future of flexible, usable, no-hassle information, and that's a critical value to establish to users who have other options.

The Bottom Line: Reality for Modern Libraries

Here's the healthiest way to look at this big pile of complexity and its attendant worry: A public website is like a public bathroom, and sooner or later, somebody's going to make a mess on the floor. Another patron might see it and be horrified. A prominent politician might see it and be noisily scandalized. Someone might even claim to have been injured by it. But the reality is that there is no 100 percent effective way to ensure that nobody every makes a mess on the floor, or that nobody ever sees it, or is scandalized by it, or steps in it. It's going to happen someday as a part of being public.

And when it does, any time spent on mess-proofing, mess-detection squads, the mess avoidance committee, or the mess remediation policy won't have helped you. It happened; clean it up and move on. Policies can't keep things from happening, and not even bathroom terms of use, under which, by entering the stall, the user agrees to place any deposits solely in the provided receptacle, will keep that mess off the floor.

Viewed through this lens, your policies and procedures are not about prevention, but about recovery; detailing not what should and should not happen, but how the organization will react not if, but when it does happen. Most policy is anxiety avoidance; good policy plots a course out of anxiety.

Remember, anyone can make a mess on anything for any reason. But having some reasonable expectations in advance about where the mess normally gets made and what might happen can help your organization—not to prevent the mess from coming, but from being paralyzed by the worry that a mess might be made. We also need to remember that people have been messing up libraries for as long as there have been libraries, and this isn't some brave new unprecedented world of things where a mess can be made; it's just the next frontier for the same old mess.

Libraries can no longer trade on their authority. Whether we know more than our patrons or not, that is no longer something most people hope to find at the library. It's critical for twenty-first-century libraries to embrace the opportunities that user-contributed content offers, for they can give us more than we could ever create ourselves, and while much of it may be rough, there are diamonds in that rough that we would never find even if we went looking in the closets and attics of our communities.

The catch, as ever, is to strike a balance between meeting the expectations of the modern Web user, assuring the administration that the library is carefully exercising stewardship of its resources, and assuaging the fears of counsel and other risk managers by illustrating how much of this risk the library has been bearing for decades without incident. It's not easy, but it can be done, and hopefully the above has illustrated a route to reach compromise.

The world is changing. Jetpacks are just around the corner, I'm sure of it. Opportunity is everywhere, and while it's not without exposure, not all exposure is additional risk, especially when anyone can sue anyone for anything. As content, media, and copyright continue to be transformed by the information revolution, libraries are hanging on a precipice; this is no time to get hung up on the edge cases.

Chapter 4

Internet Filtering

Sarah Houghton-Jan

Abstract

Laws and library practices regarding content filtering have a significant impact on library customers' constitutionally protected access to information, their privacy, and their right to free speech. Libraries have a responsibility to be informed about relevant laws, technologies, and best practices in order to protect the intellectual freedom rights of our customers in an increasingly digital information landscape. This chapter of Privacy and Freedom of Information in 21st-Century Libraries *aims to help librarians begin to fulfill that responsibility.*

Internet filtering, also referred to as content filtering or censorware, is one of the most pervasive and recurring intellectual freedom challenges for libraries worldwide. For some libraries, and indeed some entire countries, there is no question of whether or not to filter—filters in libraries are simply mandated by the government. In the United States, however, there is still at least a cursory nod to intellectual freedom and privacy from our governing agencies. But filtering in the United States is tied to optional, and tempting, library funding.

A divisive issue in libraries, the question of content filtering is central to our communities' future of information access. Content filtering involves values of a fundamental nature, so any solution results in parties feeling that they are giving up something of profound importance. There is no compromise, no middle ground. The American Library Association (ALA) has stated unequivocally that any type of restriction on a person's, including a child's, access to any type of content is unacceptable. The ALA *Library Bill of Rights* says very clearly: "A person's right to use a library should not be denied or abridged because of origin, age, background, or views."[1] To the ALA and many librarians, content filters of any kind are antithetical to the mission of the library to provide free and open access to all information.

Simply put, filters block legitimate content with no threat to children while simultaneously allowing access to graphic sexual content that does pose a threat. Internet filters effect content-based restrictions on free speech. To most librarians, especially to those who champion intellectual freedom, Internet filters are constitutionally unacceptable for use in libraries, or anywhere else for that matter.

Laws and Court Cases Related to Internet Filters

There are several laws and court cases that affect library use of Internet filters. Details about the court cases are explicated in the online sources listed in the gray box.

- First Amendment of the United States Constitution
- Child Online Protection Act (COPA) [passed as law, but overturned in courts as unconstitutional]
- Children's Internet Protection Act (CIPA)
- state or local codes
- *ACLU v. Gonzalez*
- *ACLU v. Miller*
- *ACLU v. Reno*
- *ALA v. Pataki*
- *ALA v. U.S. Department of Justice*
- *Mainstream Loudoun v. Board of Trustees of Loudoun County Library*
- *Bradburn v. North Central Regional Library District*
- *United States v. American Library Association*

> **Court Cases Relevant to Internet Filters in Libraries**
>
> *ACLU v. Gonzalez*
>
> www.paed.uscourts.gov/documents/opinions/07D0346P.pdf
>
> *ACLU v. Miller*
>
> www.aclu.org/technology-and-liberty/federal-district-court-decision-aclu-v-miller
>
> *ACLU v. Reno II*
>
> www.aclu.org/technology-and-liberty/feature-aclu-v-reno-ii
>
> *ALA v. Pataki*
>
> www.aclu.org/technology-and-liberty/feature-ala-v-pataki
>
> *ACLU v. U.S. Department of Justice and Reno v. ACLU*
>
> www.ciec.org
>
> *Mainstream Loudoun v. Board of Trustees of Loudoun County Library*
>
> www.tomwbell.com/NetLaw/Ch04/Loudoun.html
>
> *Preliminary Injunction Against Child Online Protection Act and Judge Lowell Reed's Decision*
>
> www.aclu.org/technology-and-liberty/judge-reeds-memorandum-granting-temporary-restraining-order-aclu-v-reno-ii
>
> *United States v. American Library Association (CIPA)*
>
> http://caselaw.lp.findlaw.com/scripts/getcase.pl?court=US&vol=000&invol=02-361

These laws and cases should be consulted for further information about local statutes related to Internet filtering, the application of CIPA, and the constitutional limitations placed on filtering implementations.

Technology of Filters

Content filters can be extremely powerful. Filters today employ artificial intelligence, image recognition, and complex keyword analysis algorithms to an extremely granular level. Filters still cannot successfully evaluate and determine the actual content, context, and intent of Web content of various media types—text, still images, video, audio, and more. As a result, filter performance is highly dependent on the program's artificial intelligence content recognition and any possible administrative human intervention, as well as the chosen settings and features.

All filters function by filtering content based on some combination of the domain, IP address, keyword, and file type. Because the amount and dispersion of the content on the Internet is growing so quickly, filtering products start with a list of domains (website address) and IP addresses (where those websites are hosted) and add into the equation some element of the content (trigger words, phrases, file types, etc.).

Products that filter based on domains and IP addresses typically use a search engine (Google in almost every documented case) to run canned searches for trigger words or phrases, such as "sex videos." That results list is then run through an algorithm that creates a blacklist of blocked pages for that topic or subject matter. Other algorithms block entire domains or IP addresses. Some companies have a staff member spot-check the auto-generated list for errors, but many have no human intervention at all. These domain blacklists generally include 250,000–2,000,000 domains or IP addresses, which are then blocked by the filtering software when a user attempts to access them.

Of paramount intellectual freedom concern to libraries is the methodology behind how content is classified in the filtering software. The automated classification processes and the whitelists and blacklists that filtering software companies develop are ferociously protected and never made publicly available to their customers. Filtering software companies do not tell their customers the types of things or what specific sites they block in each category. No examples are given, and no information beyond a one- or two-sentence description is offered for any company's product. Their methodology is considered a company trade secret and vital to their continued success.

There are numerous workarounds to content filters that experienced users will fast-learn and easily use. Sites like Peacefire.org are dedicated to helping individuals get around filters. Another method of bypassing filters is through proxy servers, such as Psiphon and StupidCensorship. Some filtering sites therefore choose to filter proxy-avoidance sites, URL translators, and other workaround sites. This raises a new and wholly different intellectual freedom concern beyond the protection of children from sexually explicit material. Many political dissidents and others attempting to hide their identities or locations (sometimes not for wholly idealistic reasons) use these tools as a way to mask their information from government agencies and others seeking to do them harm. As a result, by disallowing the use of these sites in our public libraries, libraries have made it impossible for this group of users to gain access to the tools they need, sometimes for life-or-death reasons.

Every single filtering software program works differently. What the end user sees is different. What the site administrator sees is different. What flexibility exists is different. It is of the utmost importance that libraries considering these products review all of the various factors at play in deciding if a product can work for them, and if so, which product will meet their needs the best.

Filter Accuracy

The accuracy of filters is key to the discussion of how Internet filters work in libraries, and everywhere else for that matter. All filters overblock (incorrectly blocking something unobjectionable) and underblock (incorrectly allowing something objectionable). The question is: how much do they do both, and is that failure rate an acceptable cost?

In filter accuracy studies from 2001 to 2008 (none were done in 2009-2010), the average accuracy success rating of all the tests combined is 78.347 percent. This means that on average, 78.347 percent of the time, the filtering software did what it was supposed to do. Bear in mind that these studies measure only text content, with only one exception of a study that examined filtering efficacy on images.[2]

If you look only at other studies done from 2007 to 2008 to get the best of the most recent software, we see a nominally higher accuracy percentage—83.316 percent—but the number of studies is limited and therefore leaves a larger margin for error. While filters may be getting a little better . . . they're still wrong at least 17 percent of the time for text content, and wrong 54 percent of the time on image content.[3]

An interesting study was done on the effectiveness of home computer Internet filters in preventing unwanted exposure of children to harmful material. The researchers found through a longitudinal study that "the use of filtering and blocking software was associated with a modest reduction (40%) in unwanted exposure, suggesting that it may help but is far from foolproof."[4]

Again and again, studies show that content is both overblocked and underblocked at consistent and equivalent rates, no matter what filter or what settings. Seventeen percent of the time, content is overblocked (i.e., benign sites are blocked incorrectly). Seventeen percent of the time, content is underblocked (i.e., sites deemed "bad" get through anyway).

The lesson that this teaches our regular Internet users is this: when you come to the library, your Internet use is going to often be blocked, usually incorrectly, and we won't tell you why. The lesson that this teaches to our hardcore Internet adult site users is this: try, try again. Examining those statistics, ask yourself as an information professional if an overall accuracy rating of 83 percent is okay for websites? If an average accuracy rating of 46 percent is okay for images?

Privacy and Filters

Filtering provides several challenges to the library's key principle of personal privacy and privacy of information needs. Before considering the implementation of filters or reassessing a current implementation, libraries need to consider issues of data collection, library privacy policies, confidentiality of information needs, and alternatives to filters.

The very nature of filtering software means that there are vast libraries of data about users' Web and other computer use habits. Libraries need to find out from filtering product vendors what information the vendors are collecting about users' surfing habits, if and how that information is connected to their computer session login or patron record, if the filtering company has access to that information, if the data is retained on the library's servers, and if so for how long and in what format. As we are mindful about other user data, so should we be with this data. Whatever can be not collected, should be not collected. Whatever data can be anonymized, should be anonymized. Whatever data is left should be protected solemnly, and access to that data should be extremely limited.

A big part of libraries' campaigns for Internet use safety and privacy has been to put Internet use policies into place. An associated policy has been the library privacy policy, largely created by libraries in response to the PATRIOT Act. Library privacy policies dictate what a library will do or not do with a customer's data. Most state what information is collected and saved, how or where it is stored, and who can access it under what circumstances (e.g., a subpoena). The utilization of filters should create an added section to library privacy policies. Libraries need to state what information they are collecting about users and who has access to it.

Another impact of filters on privacy in libraries is a user's need for confidentiality when it comes to his or her information needs. One of the principles on which libraries pride themselves is that anyone can ask a library staff person any question, access any resource, and the library will not freely make that information available to their friends or law enforcement (without a subpoena). Their information needs are secure and private when it comes to the library's physical collections and library-selected digital collections, and most librarians believe that this principle should extend into the library's de facto digital collection: the Internet. However, if a library places filters on computers and requires a library staff member to intervene to approve a blocked site, then this confidentiality evaporates. The user has to tell the library staff member what he or she wants to look at. And that information might pass through several library staff members' hands before it makes it into the whitelist database or even through some of the filtering company's employees' hands as they make that change for the library instead. Customers with sensitive needs are very unlikely to be willing to ask a library staff member to unblock a site for them about, for example, male impotence or divorce. By requiring staff intervention, libraries violate the principle of confidentiality of information needs, a key tenet of library user rights.

Beyond library policies for privacy and Internet use, there some alternatives to Internet filtering in use in the library world that help to protect users' privacy, and which should be considered in the place of or in addition to filtering software. These alternatives are almost universally used by libraries that choose to not filter their users' access.

Libraries can teach classes to self-registered attendees in the library, at school visits, during parent nights, and during visits to local Rotary Clubs and similar organizations. Internet safety for children, privacy, data security, and social media and privacy are common topics. Helping to protect users' information is an important role of the library, and teaching users best practices is the most successful way to encourage data security and privacy.

Privacy screens can help, although in only a limited way, to keep what users are looking at on their screens private. Research at the San José Public Library into various types and brands of screens found that their physical zones of successful blocking behind the monitor were quite small. For all of the screens SJPL tested, one could see what users were viewing for about a 30 degree angle area behind them.[5] Thus, privacy screens should be utilized only with the caveat that the computer screen is still visible to those seeking to view it.

Libraries can also consider the placement of computers. Placing computers in isolated areas will allow users to maintain their privacy. Placing computers in busy walkways with the screens facing out creates a problem, as they are very visible.

Some libraries create profiles that are age-based, allowing users who are under 18, or under 12, to log in only on certain computers. Placing children's computers in an isolated area can help to protect the data that children are entering on the computer as fewer adults are likely to be wandering that area.

None of these is an ultimate solution for protecting user information. The library should do what it can to coach users to protect their information and privacy, but still rely on individual responsibility for data security and privacy.

Intellectual Freedom and Filters

Four of the six statements of principle in the American Library Association's *Library Bill of Rights* are relevant to Internet filtering (emphasis the author's):

- Materials should not be excluded because of the origin, background, or views of those contributing to their creation.
- Libraries should challenge censorship in the fulfillment of their responsibility to provide information and enlightenment.
- Libraries should cooperate with all persons and groups concerned with resisting abridgment of free expression and free access to ideas.
- A person's right to use a library should not be denied or abridged because of origin, age, background, or views.[6]

If a librarian believes in the ALA *Library Bill of Rights* and is willing to stand up for these core professional values, then it would appear that in no case is it acceptable for a library to filter the Internet for any group of people. Internet filters exclude material. By excluding material, they are censoring information and abridging free access to ideas. Libraries should work with other groups concerned with the same issue. And finally, and perhaps most poignant, no one's library use or access to information should be affected by his or her age. According to the *Library Bill of Rights*, it is not acceptable to lessen a user's library access because of the individual's age, and filtering Internet access based on age is definitely lessening access. These are the principles that we librarians in the United States have agreed to champion. If we take this document seriously, then any Internet filtering implementation or legislation should continue to be a key point of contention for all ALA members.

A key issue brought up in the court decisions surrounding CIPA and Internet filtering in libraries is the idea of "selection versus censorship." Some courts contend that installing filters is equal to library selection of materials, or collection development decisions, and that each individual library has the right to make those selection decisions and they do not violate First Amendment rights as a result.

I'd like to deconstruct that statement. Installing filters on your public access library computers is a bit like outsourcing to a single company all of your collection development—that one entity will be making all collection decisions about what is immediately accessible and what is not. You might be able to tweak it a little bit, but your default collection is already decided by someone else. Even more, because the process of selection for what sites are blocked by the filter is 99 percent automated by a computer script, installing a filter is like entrusting the entirety of your collection development to an automated computer system instead of to human beings.

If you'll permit me to carry the analogy a little further, like requiring users to use interlibrary loan to get an item that is not in your collection, Internet filters require users to ask a librarian to override the system so that they can access an item that is not in the library's "acceptable" Internet collection. And like the many users who are stopped by the hassle and delay of ILL, users of filtered library computers are stopped in their tracks by the hassle and delay of the filter's big "no, no, no!" warning when they try to access something that may very well be a totally legitimate site that in fact does not violate the library's policies.

There is sufficient legal precedent that libraries cannot legally adopt or enforce private rating schemes, which is what Internet filtering software uses. The American Library Association states that "when libraries restrict access based on content ratings developed and applied by a filtering vendor, sometimes with no knowledge of how these ratings are applied or what sites have been restricted, they are delegating their public responsibility to a private agency."[7] The legality of this issue is still being fought out in the courts, most recently in Washington State, where it was decided that Internet filters are not censorship because filtering is equivalent to collection development[8] (see directly above for contradicting argument). There are contrasting court opinions, and the issues will likely be fought out for a long time, or until the Congress passes new legislation.

Deciding what is on the software's core blacklists and whitelists is up to machines and filtering software company staff who are untrained on freedom of information, constitutional issues, or best practices for information objectivity. Library staff have the ability, usually, to add pages and domains to the whitelist or blacklist. Subjectivity is a part of human nature, so who on the library staff gets to decide what is bad and what isn't? What is the library's procedure for adding something to either list? How do we "select" in the future when the software rolls out updated lists? How do we know how the software makers decide what gets blocked and what doesn't? How do we ensure that this is an objective process, an accurate process? The answer: we cannot.

How do we know that the morals and values of the company CEO aren't making their way into the software's lists, in violation of the library's core principles of equal and open access to all ideas and points of view? For example, San José Public Library's research showed that WebSense filtering categories have subcategories, some of which are divided into political positions. With one click you can block only pro-choice or only pro-life websites or choose to block only occult or nontraditional religious sites.[9] X-Stop was shown to block sites such as the Quaker website and the National Journal of Sexual Orientation Law,[10] while CYBERsitter blocked sites like the National Organization for Women.[11] Libraries have a duty to ask ourselves what values are already in the software's algorithms, and what procedures build the blacklists.

Internet filters do not constitute selection, and paying for the Internet does not constitute paying for pornography, according to past ALA President Mitch Freedman. Freedman wrote, "Just like buying the dictionary doesn't just pay for certain words, paying to provide public Internet access doesn't just pay for just the best or worst of this amazing communications and information tool. We don't rip out unsavory interviews in *Rolling Stone* or edit photography books—why would we cut swathes through the Internet? . . . The filters cut with all of the subtlety of a meat-cleaver."[12]

Many feel that automated artificial intelligence selection of what content to block does not constitute selection. Chris Hansen of the ACLU is often quoted as saying that mandating filters in libraries is like mandating that some stranger randomly pull books off shelves and make them unavailable, all the while not telling librarians or customers why the books aren't available or what books were pulled.

Another issue to consider is the Big Brother Factor. It's well-demonstrated that users behave differently if they feel they are being watched. Libraries must consider what effect filters will have on their users. Users may not try to access sites they think might be blocked, worrying that their use is being tracked. Users may not even try to go to that site about incontinence, or the video showing women how to conduct a breast self-exam. At libraries that filter, library customers report often not being willing to ask for something to be unblocked for them because they are embarrassed as the library has already deemed what they want to be unsavory. We must ask ourselves: how many of our library customers walk away without the information they need because of the Big Brother Factor?

Finally, the influence of outside lobbying groups on local Internet filtering policies in libraries should not be understated. Some groups, such as the Values Advocacy Council and SafeLibraries.org, have local affiliate organizations that they expect to get Internet filters into local school and public libraries. These groups provide local politicians in their like-minded political party with template proposals for Internet filtering ballot measures, city council resolutions, policy changes, and so on. This often provides the politician, in his or her mind, with a clear winning platform for the next election. These prewritten policy-change templates require the politician to insert only his or her city, school, or county name. With such an easily presented fast lane to election supremacy, libraries and intellectual freedom advocates must stand vigilant and constantly remind politicians that their constituents include people who believe in the right of choice, not only people who believe in their right to remove everyone else's choice.

Additional Library Challenges with Filtering

There are several additional issues and challenges that libraries face with Internet filtering, including the question of libraries acting *in loco parentis*, the false sense of security created by filters, the de-emphasis on education from our government leaders and the courts, the need for Internet use policies, and finally the cost-benefit analysis of complying with CIPA.

Libraries often challenge Internet filtering, as they challenge limiting children's access to certain books, as a problem of parents wanting the library to act *in loco parentis*—in the place of the parents. Libraries have traditionally not wished to fill that role, instead tending toward education of library users about the issues so they can decide for themselves. Libraries promote that only free and open Internet access can address both the First Amendment rights of youth and the right of the parent to guide his or her children.

Filters are also believed to create a false sense of security for people using them, or for parents whose children are using the filtered computers. Looking back at our accuracy ratings for Internet filters (83 percent for text, 46 percent for images), one might imagine that the number of sites or images that would be harmful to minors that still make it through the filters would give proponents pause. For some parents and guardians, placing a filter on a computer is like an announcement saying, "Hey, we have free professionally supervised daycare at the library—just plunk the kid down at the computer!" The parent is left with a sense that his or her child will definitely not encounter any unwanted material on the computer, and the parent may not even consider what unobjectionable material that the child needs might get blocked. Thus, installing filters might be associated with even more exposure to harmful material because the parents will give the children free rein and latitude to use the computers—which still have access to this harmful material. This false sense of security is of great concern to librarians and can be combated only with parent and library user education about what the filters can and cannot do.

There has been little emphasis on education of library users about Internet content, safe searching, and filter capabilities. Most libraries that do not filter have some sort of Internet safety classes for customers (usually geared toward parents), as well as literature and webpages devoted to educating customers about the reality of safety online and access to adult and other unwanted materials.

Numerous panels assigned to explore the issue of obscene Web content and Internet filters have returned with recommendations for additional education of citizens as an alternative or addition to the filtering technology itself. The National Telecommunications and Information Administration recommended in its 2003 study of Internet filtering technology that "technology protection measures are most effective when teachers and educational institutions can customize technology and use it in connection with other strategies and tools."[13] The NTIA also recommended "new legislative language that would clarify CIPA's existing 'technology protection measure' language to ensure that technology protection measures include more than just blocking and filtering technology."[14] This education about other strategies and tools and modification to CIPA language have never happened, and we still have only the CIPA language mandating filters as the sole protection measure against accidental child exposure to harmful materials.

Libraries and the American Library Association openly share their Internet use policies, usually on the library's website. ALA and other organizations have chimed in with recommendations on what makes a good Internet use policy. ALA's "Libraries and the Internet Toolkit" is an excellent place to start if your library needs to write or update your own Internet use policy. CIPA itself also outlines several required elements for the Acceptable Use Policies (usually called "Internet Access Policies" by libraries) that are mandated in the law.

- The policy must have offered the opportunity for public input.
- The policy must state the use of filters.
- It must offer ways to monitor student use of the Internet.
- It must provide for a way to block or filter visual depictions of material that is obscene.
- It must discuss safety and security principles for minors with electronic communications.
- It must discuss responses to access by minors to inappropriate sites, and it must discuss responses to hacking or other unauthorized workarounds to the software.[15]

ALA's Libraries and the Internet Toolkit
www.ala.org/ala/aboutala/offices/oif/iftoolkits/litoolkit/default.cfm

One additional key issue to consider is that the policy is not just about the Internet—it's about the use of your public computers, and you may also choose to include the use of your public network as well, including all of those laptop users. If so, the policy's name and context needs to change in accordance with its expanded reach, perhaps to the "Library Computer, Network, and Internet Use Policy."

Libraries, whether they are currently filtering or not, may also wish to conduct a cost-benefit analysis comparing the cost of Internet filters to the funding they receive in exchange through ERATE, LSTA, or other federal grants. The money received for filtering is fairly straightforward in nature. Figuring out the true costs of filtering requires a bit of math ability. We must look at not only the cost of the filtering software itself, but the cost of support and maintenance, any server or network slowdown cost, the staff time it takes to be trained plus any staff time spent unblocking or blocking sites, IT staff time to maintain the system if necessary, the cost in staff time and marketing about the library's policy, and any other costs you might encounter. Beyond the straight math, we must also consider that filters can cause the library customers to lose access to information, lose time as they work around the filters, and lose confidence in the library's relevance and ability to meet their needs. Those costs are incalculable.

Most libraries discover that they actually lose a substantial amount of money when they choose to install filters. Government commissions often see ERATE as free money and do not see the hidden implementation costs it takes to comply with ERATE requirements. The San José Public Library had $35,000 to gain in ERATE funding by implementing filters. Estimated start-up costs for the filtering software technology, staff training, hardware, and software totaled $400,000 per year with ongoing annual costs of $275,00–$300,000. Therefore, for our library, filtering for the purposes of ERATE funding was not a net-profitable situation by any means.[16]

As all librarians know, libraries that are well-funded have always provided better collections to their users. The Internet, however, provides an opportunity to level that playing field. This opportunity is stymied by CIPA because installing filters requires libraries to pay money to, in fact, reduce their collection's size by limiting access to the Internet's resources. Poor communities can either turn down ERATE funding and preserve the size of their Internet "collection" through unfettered access, or they can accept funding and spend money on filters to reduce access. Sadly, the poorer the community, the more it has to lose as ERATE discounts increase in proportion to the library's financial challenges. Additionally, poorer communities fear lawsuits even more and sometimes choose to filter simply in order to avoid the possibility of litigation from religious and other special interest groups. As a result, it is often our most economically disadvantaged communities that find themselves filtering out of a monetary obligation. It is also these communities that would most benefit from unfettered access to the Internet to help level that intellectual and societal playing field.

Conclusion

Intellectual freedom advocates believe that Internet filtering is censorship. Proponents for filters believe that Internet filtering protects our children. I encourage both sides to examine the data on filters' effectiveness. I believe that such data analysis will change the debate entirely, from a philosophical debate to one of technological capabilities and the costs that are incurred with imperfect technologies. Sadly, the technology has not caught up with our expectations for how it should work. Until it does, the debate about Internet filtering in libraries needs to change from one purely about philosophical principles to one also including the hard data demonstrating these filters' serious flaws. Providing access to information, a library's primary goal, cannot be accomplished through draconian governmental regulation over libraries restricting access. Instead, librarians, parents, and thoughtful individuals everywhere in our communities should work together to find ways to educate, prepare, and support our community members as digital citizens.

Notes

1. American Library Association, *Library Bill of Rights*, adopted June 19, 1939; amended Oct. 14, 1944; June 18, 1948; Feb. 2, 1961; June 27, 1967; and Jan. 23, 1980; www.ala.org/ala/issuesadvocacy/intfreedom/library bill/index.cfm (accessed Aug. 31, 2010).
2. Sarah Houghton-Jan and the San José Public Library, "*Internet Filtering Software Tests: Barracuda, CyberPatrol, FilterGate, & WebSense,*" April 2, 2008; www.sjlibrary.org/about/sjpl/commission/agen0208_report.pdf (accessed Aug. 31, 2010).
3. Paul Resnick, "Exhibit D: Declaration of Resnick," Feb. 4, 2008; http://filteringfacts.files.wordpress.com/2008/02/bradburn_04_05_08_resnick_report.pdf (accessed Aug. 31, 2010).
4. Kimberly J. Mitchell, David Finkelhor, and Janis Wolak, "The Exposure of Youth to Unwanted Sexual Material on the Internet: A National Survey of Risk, Impact, and Prevention," *Youth and Society* 34, no. 3, (March 2003): 330.
5. Jane Light and the San Jose Public Library, "Policy Options and Staff Report Relating to Internet Filtering Proposal and Computer Use at San Jose Public Libraries," May 27, 2008; www.sjlibrary.org/about/sjpl/commission/internet_filtering_proposal.pdf (accessed Aug. 31, 2010).
6. ALA, *Library Bill of Rights*.
7. American Library Association, "Guidelines and Considerations for Developing a Public Library Internet Use Policy," rev. Nov. 2000, www.ala.org/ala/issues advocacy/banned/challengeslibrarymaterials/essential preparation/guidelinesinternetuse/index.cfm (accessed Aug. 31, 2010).
8. Supreme Court of the State of Washington, Opinion Information Sheet for Bradburn v. North Central Regional Library District, www.mrsc.org/mc/courts/supreme/Slip%20Opinions/822000MAJ.htm (accessed Aug. 31, 2010).
9. Houghton-Jan and SJPL, "Internet Filtering Software Tests."
10. Jonathan Wallace, "The Mind of a Censor," *Ethical Spectacle* 3, no. 11 (Nov. 1997); www.spectacle.org/cs/

burt.html (accessed Aug. 31, 2010)
11. Bennett Haselton. "CYBERsitter: Where Do We Not Want You to Go Today?" published Nov. 5, 1996, on Peacefire.org, last updated Dec. 11, 1996, reprinted on *the Ethical Spectacle* website, www.spectacle.org/alert/peace.html (accessed Aug. 31, 2010).
12. 12. Mitch Freedman, "Educating about Internet Filtering," *American Libraries* 34, no. 3 (March 2003): 5.
13. U.S. Department of Commerce, National Telecommunications and Information Administration, "Report to Congress: Children's Internet Protection Act (Pub. L. 106-554): Study of Technology Protection Measures in Section 1703," Aug. 2003, 34.
14. Ibid.
15. U.S. Department of Commerce, National Telecommunications and Information Administration, "Report to Congress: Children's Internet Protection Act (Pub. L. 106-554): Study of Technology Protection Measures in Section 1703," Aug. 2003, 32–34.
16. Light and SJPLibrary, "Policy Options and Staff Report."

Resources for Further Information

Adams, Helen. "Privacy and Confidentiality: Now More Than Ever Youngsters Need to Keep Their Library Use Under Wraps." *American Libraries* 33, no. 10 (Nov. 2002): 44–46, 48.

American Library Association. "Guidelines and Considerations for Developing a Public Library Internet Use Policy." Rev. Nov. 2000, www.ala.org/ala/issuesadvocacy/banned/challengeslibrarymaterials/essentialpreparation/guidelinesinternetuse/index.cfm.

———. "Libraries and the Internet Toolkit." Upd. Dec. 1, 2003. www.ala.org/ala/aboutala/offices/oif/iftoolkits/litoolkit/default.cfm.

Ayre, Lori Bowen. "Filtering and Filter Software." *Library Technology Reports* 40, no. 2 (March–April 2004).

———. "Infopeople Project How-To Guides: Filtering the Internet." Sept. 19, 2002. Infopeople Project website, http://infopeople.org/resources/filtering/index.html.

———. "Internet Filtering Options Analysis: An Interim Report." San Mateo, CA: Infopeople Project, May 2001. http://statelibrary.dcr.state.nc.us/hottopic/cipa/InternetFilter_Rev1.pdf.

Brooks, Joyce and Jody K. Howard. "What Would You Do? School Library Media Centers and Intellectual Freedom." *Colorado Libraries* 28, no. 3 (Fall 2002): 17–19.

Brunessaux, Sylvie, et al. *Report for the European Commission: Review of Currently Available COTS Filtering Tools.* Brussels: European Commission, 2001.

Commission on Child Online Protection. "Report to Congress." Oct. 20, 2000.

Consumers Union. "Digital Chaperones for Kids." *Consumer Reports* 66, no. 3 (March 2001): 20–22.

———. "Filtering Software: Better But Still Fallible." *Consumer Reports* 70, no. 6 (June 2005): 36–38. http://hs.yarmouth.k12.me.us/Pages/YSD_YHSTechnology/PResources/ConsumerReports.FilteringSo.pdf.

Edelmen, Ben. *Sites Blocked by Internet Filtering Programs: Expert Report for Multnoman County Public Library et al. v. United States of America et al.* Cambridge, MA: Ben Edelman, 2002.

eTesting Labs. *Corporate Content Filtering Performance and Effectiveness Testing: Competitive Comparison between Websense Enterprise v4.3, SurfControl SuperScout for Windows NT/2000 and Secure Computing SmartFilter 3.01.* March 2002. http://web.archive.org/web/20030406232751/www.websense.com/whyqualitymatters/etestinglabs-fullreport.pdf.

———. *U.S. Department of Justice: Updated Web Content Filtering Software Comparison.* Oct. 2001. http://web.archive.org/web/20030727105727/http:/veritest.com/clients/reports/usdoj/usdoj.pdf

Finnell, Cory, for the Certus Consulting Group. *Internet Filtering Accuracy Review.* Washington, DC: Department of Justice. 2001. http://filteringfacts.files.wordpress.com/2007/11/cipa_trial_finnell_ex_report.pdf.

Freedman, Mitch. "Educating about Internet Filtering." *American Libraries* 34, no. 3 (March 2003): 5.

Greenberg, Pam. "Children and the Internet: Laws Relating to Filtering, Blocking, and Usage Policies in Schools and Libraries." Updated Dec. 28, 2009. National Conference of State Legislatures website, www.ncsl.org/IssuesResearch/TelecommunicationsInformationTechnology/StateInternetFilteringLaws/tabid/13491/Default.aspx.

Greenfield, Paul, Peter Rickwood, and Huu Cuong Tran. *Effectiveness of Internet Filtering Software Products.* Australian Broadcasting Authority. 2001.

Hamilton, Stuart. "Internet Accessible Information and Censorship, Intellectual Freedom and Libraries—a Global Overview." *IFLA Journal* 28, no. 4 (July 2002): 190–197.

Haselton, Bennett. "CYBERsitter: Where Do We Not Want You to Go Today?" Published Nov. 5, 1996, on Peacefire.org, last updated Dec. 11, 1996, reprinted on *the Ethical Spectacle* website, www.spectacle.org/alert/peace.html.

———. *Report on the Accuracy Rate of FortiGuard.* American Civil Liberties Union, Aug. 3, 2007. http://filteringfacts.files.wordpress.com/2007/11/bradburn_haselton_report.pdf.

Heins, Marjorie, Christina Cho, and Ariel Feldman. *Internet Filters: A Public Policy Report,* 2nd ed. New York: Brennan Center for Justice, NYU School of Law, 2006. www.fepproject.org/policyreports/filters2.pdf.

Himma, Kenneth Einar. "What If Libraries Really Had the 'Ideal Filter'?" *Alki* 19, no. 1 (March 2003): 29–30.

Houghton-Jan, Sarah, and the San José Public Library. "*Internet Filtering Software Tests: Barracuda, CyberPatrol, FilterGate, & WebSense.*" April 2, 2008. www.sjlibrary.org/about/sjpl/commission/agen0208_report.pdf.

Janes, Joseph. *Expert Report of Joseph Janes.* American Civil Liberties Union, Oct. 15, 2001. www.aclu.org/FilesPDFs/janesreport.pdf.

Light, Jane, and the San Jose Public Library. "Policy Options and Staff Report Relating to Internet Filtering Proposal and Computer Use at San Jose Public Libraries." May 27, 2008. www.sjlibrary.org/about/sjpl/commission/internet_filtering_proposal.pdf.

Marshall, Richard. "The Polarizing Effect of Internet Filters: Should ALA Take a Position?" *Mississippi Libraries* 65, no. 4 (Winter 2001):109–110.

Minow, Mary. "Who Pays for Free Speech? The Cost of Defending the First Amendment is Diverting Scarce Resources from Library Services." *American Libraries* 34, no. 2 (Feb. 2003): 34–38.

Mitchell, Kimberly J., David Finkelhor, and Janis Wolak. "The Exposure of Youth to Unwanted Sexual Material on the Internet: A National Survey of Risk, Impact, and Prevention." *Youth and Society* 34, no. 3 (March 2003): 330–358.

Net Protect. Report on the Evaluation of the Final Version of the NetProtect Product. 2004. http://ec.europa.eu/information_society/activities/sip/archived/docs/pdf/projects/netproject_2_d5_2.pdf.

Online Policy Group and the Electronic Freedom Foundation. *Internet Blocking in Public Schools: A Study on Internet Access in Educational Institutions.* San Francisco: Online Policy Group, June 2003. www.onlinepolicy.org/access/blocking/net_block_report/net_block_report.pdf.

Resnick, Paul. "Exhibit D: Declaration of Resnick." Feb. 4, 2008. http://filteringfacts.files.wordpress.com/2008/02/bradburn_04_05_08_resnick_report.pdf.

Rideout, Victoria, Caroline Richardson, and Paul Resnick. *See No Evil: How Internet Filters Affect the Search for Online Health Information.* Menlo Park, CA: Kaiser Family Foundation, Dec. 12, 2002. www.kff.org/entmedia/3294-index.cfm.

Shanks, Thomas E., and Barry J. Stenger. *Access, Internet, and Public Libraries—The Effectiveness of Filtering Software: Recommendations.* Santa Clara University, 2007. www.scu.edu/ethics/practicing/focusareas/technology/libraryaccess.

Stark, Philip B. "Expert Report of Philip B. Stark, Ph.D." Department of Justice. May 8, 2006. http://filteringfacts.files.wordpress.com/2007/11/copa_trial_stark_report.pdf.

Thornburgh, Dick, and Herbert S. Lin, eds. *Youth, Pornography, and the Internet.* Washington, DC: National Academy Press, 2002. www.nap.edu/openbook.php?isbn=0309082749.

U.S. Department of Commerce, National Telecommunications and Information Administration. "Report to Congress: Children's Internet Protection Act (Pub. L. 106-554): Study of Technology Protection Measures in Section 1703." Aug. 2003.

Untangle. "Deep Throat Fight Club: Open Testing of Porn Filters." April 9, 2008. www.untangle.com/index.php?option=com_content&task=view&id=283&Itemid=1122.

Veritest. *Websense: Web Filtering Effectiveness Study.* Jan. 2006. www.lionbridge.com/NR/rdonlyres/websensecontentfilte7fmspvtsryjhojtsecqomzmiriqoefctif.pdf.

Wallace, Jonathan. "The Mind of a Censor," *Ethical Spectacle* 3, no. 11 (Nov. 1997), www.spectacle.org/cs/burt.html.

Chapter 5

Social Networking and the Library

Jason Griffey

Abstract

Much has been written in the last few years about the rise of online social networks and the assumption that this rise results in a decline in privacy. At the same time, libraries and librarians have deeply held beliefs about patron privacy, and they attempt to forestall access to the information habits of their patrons. These two conflicting stances—assisting in access to networks that potentially damage privacy while desiring to protect information about their patrons—will be the focus of this chapter of Privacy and Freedom of Information in 21st-Century Libraries.

Much has been written in the last few years about the rise of online social networks and the assumption that this rise results in a decline in privacy. Nearly every new Web property in the last three years has had some form of social connectivity in it, and even established Web brands like Google have tried (and sometimes failed) to take advantage of the newly social Net. Libraries have navigated this new terrain by creating identities for themselves, interacting with patrons within the various sites, and providing access and sometimes even training on how best to use sites like Facebook, Twitter, FriendFeed, and more. At the same time, libraries and librarians have deeply held beliefs about patron privacy, and allowing access to the information habits of their patrons is something that libraries attempt to forestall. These two conflicting stances, that of assisting in access to networks that potentially damage privacy and that of desiring to protect information about their patrons, will be the focus of this chapter.

What we consider an online social network site dates back to the early days of the Internet, with the advent of a website called SixDegrees.com in 1997.[1] The history of social networks online is, however, one of rise and fall, with one site rising in popularity only to be overtaken by another when the whims of the online audience find a reason to move. This cycle started with Friendster in 2002, moving to MySpace in 2003, and then on to the current market leader, Facebook, in 2005. As I'm writing this, it's mid-June 2010, and Facebook is expected this week to announce that it has crossed the 500 million user mark, something that no other website has ever accomplished.[2] I'm not sure that anything in history has had 500 million active participants; that's a full one-twelfth of the entire population of the planet. If Facebook were a country and its users citizens, it would be the third most populous country in the world, behind only China and India.

What makes something a social network site? Danah M. Boyd and Nicole B. Ellison in their seminal 2007 article "Social Network Sites: Definition, History, and Scholarship" define a social network site as "web-based services that allow individuals to (1) construct a public or semi-public profile within a bounded system, (2) articulate a list of other users with whom they share a connection, and (3) view and traverse their list of connections and those made by others within the system."[3] There are sites for which the entire point is the socialization and limitation or control of your information, such as MySpace and Facebook, and then there are sites that have some other central purpose like Flickr (sharing photos) and YouTube (sharing videos). There are also interest-specific or topical sites with extensive social networking features, such as LibraryThing (discussing books), Babycenter (motherhood and parenting), Ravelry (knitting and crocheting), and Disaboom (living with a disability or functional limitation). For any given hobby, at this point on the Web, there is probably a social network site that caters to it.

Social networks have grown in popularity in the last five years, with the Pew Internet reporting that 82 percent of teens 14–17 have used a social networking site.[4] The same report shows that young adults age 18–29 are also huge social network users, with 72 percent of them reporting regular use.[5] After 30, social network use drops precipitously (to 40 percent), but that is likely a generational effect and not a direct age effect; it's happening because of the time during which the people surveyed were 30 or over, and we can expect that as the current 25–29-year-olds march past the 30-year mark that average social network use will rise as well as the generation that is comfortable with them ages.

For libraries, there are two sides to the use of social networks: use by patrons and use by the library. Both of these uses of social networks are sometimes in conflict with long-held positions about patron privacy, and it isn't clear whether it's possible for libraries to both hold on to their ideals and be a part of the modern online world. Let's look at a few scenarios for specific uses of current social networks and see how they hold up to patron privacy.

The central tension between libraries and social networks is simple: a social network gains usefulness when you are identifiable (people know who you are) and you share information about yourself (people know what you like). Libraries have, for years, operated under the general guideline that both of those pieces of knowledge are no one's business but yours. The American Library Association's Code of Ethics says in its third statement, "We protect each library user's right to privacy and confidentiality with respect to information sought or received and resources consulted, borrowed, acquired or transmitted."[6] In fact the ALA Policy on Confidentiality of Library Records is so strong, I felt that I should quote it in its entirety here:

> The Council of the American Library Association strongly recommends that the responsible officers of each library, cooperative system, and consortium in the United States:
>
> 1. Formally adopt a policy that specifically recognizes its circulation records and other records identifying the names of library users to be confidential. (See also ALA Code of Ethics, Article III, "We protect each library user's right to privacy and confidentiality with respect to information sought or received, and resources consulted, borrowed, acquired or transmitted" and Privacy: An Interpretation of the Library Bill of Rights.)
> 2. Advise all librarians and library employees that such records shall not be made available to any agency of state, federal, or local government except pursuant to such process, order or subpoena as may be authorized under the authority of, and pursuant to, federal, state, or local law relating to civil, criminal, or administrative discovery procedures or legislative investigative power.
> 3. Resist the issuance of enforcement of any such process, order, or subpoena until such time as a proper showing of good cause has been made in a court of competent jurisdiction.[7]

When patrons were just checking things out from the library, and the library itself was the owner and manager of that transactional information, these rules were easy to understand. But when patrons started accessing social networking sites on library computers and using a library's network, it became difficult for the library to manage the privacy of the patron in the same way. There are significant difficulties in protecting patron information when there are several layers of networks to content with, and to top it off, some portion of the information being shared is being shared intentionally by the patron. Libraries have never tried to regulate whether patrons could voluntarily give up their own privacy . . . we don't really care if someone keeps a public list of the books he's read, as long as it is his list.

In addition to the library privacy issues, there are serious concerns among school and public libraries about the safety of minors on social networks. The same sorts of peer pressure, bullying, abuse, and other social minefields that were once confined to school hours are now extendable outside of them and onto social networks. Some libraries and school systems have chosen to limit access to social networking sites for content-based reasons, something that seems at odds with the American Library Association's *Library Bill of Rights*, especially the first three policies:

> I. Books and other library resources should be provided for the interest, information, and enlightenment of all people of the community the library serves. Materials should not be excluded because of the origin, background, or views of those contributing to their creation.
> II. Libraries should provide materials and information presenting all points of view on current and historical issues. Materials should not be proscribed or removed because of partisan or doctrinal disapproval.
> III. Libraries should challenge censorship in the fulfillment of their responsibility to provide information and enlightenment.[8]

Taken at face value, as they relate to social networks, library ethical policies can be interpreted as directly contradictory to the above privacy statements. Libraries have chosen, at times, to value privacy over access to social networks when these are in conflict. If the privacy of the patron is compromised via social networks, one possible answer is to attempt to limit access to those networks, which flies in the face of open and free access to information.

For instance, the highly publicized banning of Facebook, MySpace, and other social network sites by the Mishawaka-Penn-Harris Public Library in Indiana in 2008 was met with a huge amount of discussion online about how the library approached the issues that led to the banning. In this instance, the reasons given for banning access were all related to teen activity in the library, but the result was that social networks simply weren't available from the library.[9] Wake County, North Carolina Board of Commissioners decided in early 2007 to ban MySpace across the entirety of the public library system in the county, calling it an "attractive nuisance."[10]

In 2006, Representative Michael Fitzpatrick of Pennsylvania introduced the Deleting Online Predators Act, or DOPA, a law that would have made it necessary for libraries that received federal funding to block social networking sites from minors in the same way that the Children's Internet Protection Act requires that certain libraries filter pornographic material from their computers.[11] The rationale for the law as given in multiple interviews was to protect children from the possibility of being preyed upon by adults. The fact that social networking sites were singled out speaks to the degree to which they were misunderstood at the time and also to the conclusions to which adults will jump when presented with a medium that they do not fully understand.

Libraries, especially public libraries, continue to struggle with providing access to social networks for any number of reasons. Library boards can place great pressure on libraries to limit access to Internet resources in the same way that they can press for collection development limitations and individual book bans. It is surprising that often libraries and librarians will react less strongly to the limitation of information on the Internet and World Wide Web than they would to the limitation of print material.

The other issue at hand with social networks and libraries is whether libraries should themselves be using social networks as part of their toolbox of outreach and patron services online. Libraries have a long history of trying to effectively use any new technology that emerges for extending their services, from the rise of the bookmobile to phone reference to the huge variety of communication mechanisms now available on the Internet (instant messaging services, e-mail, blogs, wikis, etc.). It's only natural that when presented with the opportunity to put themselves in front of their patrons in a new way, libraries would experiment and see how the patrons respond.

Libraries saw several problems arise quickly with their use of social networks, specifically Facebook. The first was that, at the time libraries started experimenting, Facebook offered only "accounts" and not pages or other content types. The terms of use at the time specified that Facebook accounts were for use only by actual individuals and not by fictional characters, groups, businesses, or schools and libraries. Some libraries spent time creating accounts within Facebook, friending and being friended by patrons, pushing content into Facebook, only to literally go in one day and find their accounts gone. This just highlights issues with trusting library information and communication channels with nonlibrary controlled sources and shouldn't necessarily be seen as a condemnation of social networks in general.

The second, less-expected problem was that libraries began to see pushback from patrons about their very presence. Not just libraries, but any organization that was seen as "outside" the social circle of the patrons, was quickly identified and seen as suspect. It took some time, and some evolution of the social networks, for this reaction to change, and it appears that now the idea of organizations as parts of social networks is one that the public is comfortable with. Facebook has pages for organizations, and Twitter and other social networks simply treat libraries as if they were just another account holder.

Both of these initial problems have been solved, and libraries are fully ensconced in social networks at this point, with library mainstays like the New York Public Library, the Library of Congress, and even the ALA Library having Facebook pages. Libraries are experimenting with other social networks like Flickr and Twitter, and librarians are using nearly every social network to be found on the Net in one way or the other.

Library Facebook Pages

New York Public Library
www.facebook.com/newyorkpubliclibrary

Library of Congress
www.facebook.com/libraryofcongress

ALA Library
www.facebook.com/alalibrary

This isn't to say that there aren't ongoing issues with social networks. Facebook, the clear leader in the current social network ecosystem, continues to make decisions about privacy and data that make many people, not just librarians, uncomfortable. Through its history, Facebook has increasingly made its default privacy settings more and more public, and less and less protected.[12] At this point, Facebook has had a series of instances where it has added a new service and the default setting is for the new service to be public to the world instead of limited to just a user's network of friends. This is largely driven by a conflict of informational use for Facebook itself; it gains trust and users because it purports to limit the information you share to a limited network of friends, but that very insularity limits it to the rest of the Web. Without exposing some of your information to the Web, it is very difficult for Facebook to make money via advertising, which is still its primary method of revenue generation. So unless Facebook finds a way to get your and your patrons' information into the public, it makes less money . . . but also runs the risk of alienating users. It's a delicate balance, and one that Facebook has seemingly successfully navigated, given its growth in users.

Given the history of social networks, there will come a time when Facebook goes just a bit too far, or maybe something more attractive will come along, and the exodus to another site will begin. Or maybe the promise of a distributed social network from something like the Diaspora Project will take shape, and people will be free to develop their own networks that will all interconnect seamlessly, erasing the problems of a single point of failure that exists in something like Facebook. If this happens, it will become even more difficult to control the access to this sort of information online, since having a noncentralized site means that it will be much more difficult to find ways to limit access to the resource.

Diaspora
www.joindiaspora.com/index.html

In this all-too-short chapter, we didn't get a chance to examine all of the niche social networks that were mentioned earlier. But the same basic tensions can be found for any of them. Problems revolving around youth culture and the acceptance from adults of a new form of communication or media production and consumption can be found with any new social network. In addition to the simple generational gap, there are objective reasons at times to limit access to some forms of media for network or other infrastructure reasons; for example, some libraries limit access to YouTube not because of its content or because it's a social network, but because the bandwidth simply isn't there to support it. Understanding and exploring social networks should be well understood at this point in history for libraries. This doesn't mean that we shouldn't be very careful in how we approach and interact with them, but it does mean that we need to think of them as another information object of interest to our patrons and carefully consider how we want to deal with them. Social networks aren't going away, and the future of the Web in general is going to be largely social: libraries need to be a vibrant part of that future.

Notes

1. danah m. boyd and Nicole B. Ellison. "Social Network Sites: Definition, History, and Scholarship." Journal of Computer-Mediated Communication, vol. 13, no. 1 (2007), article 11, http://jcmc.indiana.edu/vol13/issue1/boyd.ellison.html (accessed Aug. 31, 2010).
2. Mark Zuckerberg, "500 Million Stories," Facebook Blog, July 21, 2010, http://blog.facebook.com/blog.php?post=409753352130 (accessed Sept. 24, 2010).
3. Boyd and Ellison, "Social Network Sites."
4. Amanda Lenhart, Kristen Purcell, Aaron Smith, and Kathryn Zickuhr, Social Media and Young Adults, Feb. 3, 2010, Part 3: Social Media, "Teens and Online Social Networks," Pew Internet and American Life Project, www.pewinternet.org/Reports/2010/Social-Media-and-Young-Adults/Part-3/1-Teens-and-online-social-networks.aspx?r=1 (accessed Aug. 31, 2010).
5. Ibid., Part 3: Social Media, "Adults and Social Networks," Pew Internet and American Life Project, www.pewinternet.org/Reports/2010/Social-Media-and-Young-Adults/Part-3/2-Adults-and-social-networks.aspx?r=1 (accessed Aug. 31, 2010).
6. Office for Intellectual Freedom, Intellectual Freedom Manual, 8th ed. (Chicago: American Library Association, 2010), www.ifmanual.org/codeethics/ (accessed Sept. 24, 2010).
7. American Library Association, "Policy on Confidentiality of Library Records," Jan. 20, 1971, amended July 4, 1975 and July 2, 1986, www.ala.org/ala/aboutala/offices/oif/statementspols/otherpolicies/policyconfidentiality.cfm (accessed Aug. 31, 2010).
8. American Library Association, Library Bill of Rights, adopted June 19, 1939; amended Oct. 14, 1944; June 18, 1948; Feb. 2, 1961; June 27, 1967; and Jan. 23, 1980; www.ala.org/ala/issuesadvocacy/intfreedom/librarybill/index.cfm (accessed Sept. 24, 2010).
9. Michael Stephens, "No MySpace, Facebook at Mishawaka Library," Tame the Web, March 18, 2008, http://tametheweb.com/2008/03/18/no-myspace-facebook-at-mishawaka-library/ (accessed Sept. 24, 2010).
10. Blake, "Wake County Public Libraries to Censor MySpace," March 1, 2007, http://lisnews.org/articles/07/03/01/131249.shtml (accessed Aug. 31, 2010).
11. Declan McCullagh, "Lawmakers Take Aim at Social Networking Sites," CNET News, May 11, 2006, http://news.cnet.com/2100-1028_3-6071040.html (accessed Sept. 24, 2010).
12. Matt McKeon, "The Evolution of Privacy on Facebook," http://mattmckeon.com/facebook-privacy (accessed Aug. 31, 2010); Kurt Opsahl, "Facebook's Eroding Privacy Policy: A Timeline," April 28, 2010, Electronic Frontier Foundation website, www.eff.org/deeplinks/2010/04/facebook-timeline (accessed Aug. 31, 2010).

Chapter 6

RFID in Libraries

Deborah Caldwell-Stone

Abstract

The implementation of radio frequency identification (RFID) technologies by U.S. libraries is noteworthy for the controversy that resulted when organizations like the Electronic Frontier Foundation and the ACLU protested libraries' adoption of RFID and argued that the privacy risks posed by RFID were so great that libraries should avoid adopting RFID technology altogether. Nearly a decade later, RFID is an accepted technology in libraries, thanks in part to the profession's adoption of best practices that minimize the technology's potential to erode library users' privacy.

The National Information Standards Organization (NISO) has since published a document, RFID in U.S. Libraries, that contains recommended practices intended to facilitate the use of radio frequency identification in library applications. Though the document includes privacy within its charge, it does not include or discuss the best practices adopted by the library profession.

This article reviews the controversy surrounding the use of RFID technologies in U.S. libraries and the steps taken by the library profession to resolve those issues. It evaluates and discusses the privacy recommendations made by NISO's RFID Working Group on RFID in U.S. Libraries.

Overview

Radio frequency identification technology enables the tracking and monitoring of physical items by attaching an RFID tag or transponder to an item. Each tag consists of an internal antenna and a computer chip that stores data. When the tag is scanned or interrogated by a reading device equipped with its own antenna, the tag communicates its data wirelessly via radio waves to the reader.

The range at which an RFID tag is read depends upon the tag design, the method of communication between the tag and the reader, and the radio frequency at which the RFID application operates. "Passive" tags do not have a power source and cannot transmit information unless powered by the energy contained in the radio signal transmitted by the RFID reader; the read range of passive tags is relatively short. "Active" RFID tags are powered by a battery or other power source and are able to transmit their signal over large distances.

The tags employed in library applications are high-frequency (HF) passive tags that operate at 13.56 MHz and can be read at distances from eight inches to two meters, depending on the size and the power of the antenna employed by the reader.[1] Tags are typically programmed with a unique identifier and a security bit, but can also contain other kinds of information, such as the book title, ISBN, library identifier, date and time stamps, and shelf locations.[2]

In libraries, RFID applications are used to automate circulation and collection management tasks. Systems developed by RFID vendors can now check in, sort, and deliver items to a designated shelving cart. Tags affixed to books, periodicals, CDs, DVDs, and other library items identify circulating materials, and readers can be incorporated into staff workstations, patron self-check stations, security gates, shelf readers, book drops, and automated sorting systems.[3]

RFID offers significant benefits to libraries. Because RFID tags do not require a clear line of sight and allow multiple items to be read in a stack, far less time and human effort are spent on processing materials. Patrons using RFID-enabled self-check stations and automated sorting equipment further free up library staff for essential work. Handheld RFID readers can be moved along the shelving units to read the tags attached to books on the shelves, allowing for more efficient and frequent inventory of the library's collection. And by eliminating the need for the repetitive movements required by traditional barcode scanning technology, RFID can help reduce the incidence of repetitive stress injuries among staff and the costs associated with lost time and workers' compensation payments.[4]

As of 2009, 1,500 libraries employ RFID applications in 2,500 facilities.[5]

A Controversy in Libraryland

In October 2003, the San Francisco Library Commission approved plans to adopt RFID tags to manage its circulating collection. The decision was not expected to be controversial. A few libraries had been implementing RFID for circulation and inventory management since the 1990s without much notice or controversy, including such prominent institutions as the University of Nevada at Las Vegas, Santa Clara Public Library, and the Seattle Public Library.[6] On the day of the announcement, however, the Electronic Frontier Foundation (EFF), a civil liberties group, filed a formal statement with the commission criticizing the decision. It argued that the use of RFID tags in the library would facilitate the tracking of individuals and their reading materials and infringe on library users' rights to privacy and freedom of expression.[7]

The EFF protest came soon after a hearing convened by the California State Senate in August 2003 that aired concerns about the potential of RFID to harm individuals' privacy rights.[8] The legislative hearing was spurred, in part, by news reports about several major retailers' plans to use hidden RFID tags to monitor shoppers' behavior.[9] The announcement that the San Francisco Public Library would be placing RFID tags on its books and audiovisual materials drew the attention of EFF and placed the issue of RFID and library users' privacy before the public.

Other civil liberties and privacy groups soon joined EFF's campaign to oppose the use of RFID tags in the San Francisco Public Library. In January 2004, Beth Givens of the Privacy Rights Clearinghouse and Pam Dixon of the World Privacy Forum attended the American Library Association's 2004 Midwinter Meeting with EFF's senior counsel, Lee Tien. The trio presented their concerns about the use of RFID in the library to the ALA Intellectual Freedom Committee and asked that ALA assess RFID technologies and their potential to harm library users' privacy rights.[10]

The Library Community Responds

Privacy advocates' claims that the RFID tags in libraries posed an unacceptable risk to borrowers' privacy elicited divergent responses from the library profession.

VTLS, a vendor of library RFID technologies, published a white paper setting out the arguments in favor of implementing RFID in libraries and explaining why privacy advocates' claims were unfounded. The article emphasized three main points:

- RFID tags used in library applications do not have an embedded power source and are inactive unless they are within the range of a reader.
- RFID tags used in library applications have a very short read range of 18 inches.
- RFID tags store only data that is equivalent to bar codes. No personally identifiable information is kept on the tag.[11]
- Library technology consultants, systems librarians and other vendors also defended RFID. They argued that RFID offered adequate security for library users' privacy and maintained that RFID was an inefficient and labor-intensive method for surveilling patrons' reading choices.[12]
- Other librarians and experts examining RFID were not so sanguine. They acknowledged the enormous benefits that could be realized by implementing RFID technologies in the library, but concluded that library RFID applications raised significant privacy concerns. They identified several problems:
- The security flaws that allow RFID tags to be read by any reader are part of the tag's architecture and cannot easily be remedied.
- Claims that the RFID tag's short read range prevents illicit surveillance ignore the trajectory of technology improvements; RFID readers can be expected to improve and become more powerful within a fairly short time period.
- Similarly, while the infrastructure to support surveillance of library RFID tags outside the library may not yet exist, increasing implementation of RFID technology in both government and commercial applications and the rise of pervasive and ubiquitous computing will eventually make such surveillance a realistic possibility.[13]

The core issue, in the view of these librarians, is RFID's potential to become a means of surveilling library users.[14] Any technology that facilitates surveillance of a patron's activities and reading habits raises significant ethical issues for a profession committed to protecting the library user's right to privacy.

Privacy Concerns Inherent in RFID Applications

The characteristics that make RFID tags so useful for circulation and collection management in libraries—the ability to uniquely identify a single item and transmit that data wirelessly when interrogated by a reader—are precisely the characteristics that raise significant privacy and security concerns about the use of RFID in libraries. Tags attached to books can transmit the data stored on the tag without being observed and without the knowledge of the person possessing the book. If the tag is read at different times or in different locations by a compatible reader, then the person's activities and locations can be identified, tracked, and compiled without that person's knowledge.

In commercial and retail uses of RFID tags, these privacy concerns could be addressed by deactivating or removing the tag from the item. Library RFID applications, however, require that the tag on the book remain live so that the tag can be reused to charge the book in and out of the library and to inventory the book.[15]

In 2004, electrical engineers David Molnar and David Wagner investigated the privacy risks associated with the two types of tags used for most library RFID applications, tags compliant with ISO 15693 and ISO 18000-3, the standards established by the International Standards Organization (ISO) to define the physical interface and commands for RFID tags and readers operating at a frequency of 13.56 MHz. Their research identified five possible means of compromising the privacy of library users:

- Library RFID tags do not employ passwords or other access controls, and can be read at will. Thus, any information stored on the tag can be skimmed by any RFID reader that complies with the tag's protocols. The greater the amount of information on the tag, the greater the possibility of identifying the particular book or the person in possession of it.
- Even with minimal information on the tag, a reader can be used to obtain the tag's primary identifier. The unique number can then be used to track or monitor the movement of the book attached to the tag and the person possessing it.
- One surveillance exploit acquires a tag's unique identifier in advance to create a "hotlist" of books, then monitors all tagged items leaving the library or passing through a particular checkpoint to discover who is carrying the hotlisted book.
- Tracking and hotlisting can occur even if a password or other security measure is used to secure the data on the tag. RFID tags employ a unique identifier at the hardware level, the collision avoidance ID, that prevents the tag from interfering with other tags' radio signals. The collision avoidance ID is broadcast any time a tag is interrogated by a reader and can be used to track or hotlist the tag.
- Finally, it is possible to eavesdrop on the wireless communication between the tag and the library's tag reader unless the communications are encrypted.[16]

All of these exploits require that the device used to read the RFID tag be within the tag's read range; for library RFID tags, that range is generally about two meters but can be as high as 3.5 meters, depending on the power of the reader.[17] Thus, while scenarios that envision tracking books via readers mounted to cars or aircraft are not possible, the read ranges for library RFID tags are sufficient to allow surreptitious reading by devices concealed in doorways, walls, and furnishings located in close environments.[18] And while the current lack of an RFID infrastructure attenuates the privacy threats posed by these exploits, evolving technology and the growing adoption of RFID could quickly make these threats real.[19]

Professional Ethics and Privacy-Invading Technologies

Librarians have long recognized that privacy is essential to freedom of inquiry. If individuals know or suspect that their intellectual activities are subject to examination by the government or other third parties, they are unlikely to fully exercise their constitutional right to read and receive ideas, information, and points of view.

The ALA Code of Ethics thus explicitly calls on librarians to protect the library user's right to privacy and confidentiality. This obligation requires librarians to uphold and protect the right to privacy and confidentiality in the library by adopting policies, procedures, and practices that reinforce and confirm library patrons' belief that their library use will be kept confidential and free from unauthorized scrutiny.

RFID, with its potential for compromising library users' privacy, therefore presents a significant ethical challenge for libraries. The resolution of such challenges does not require that libraries forgo or abandon new technologies. Rather, it requires librarians to seek out information about the new technology; understand its benefits, risks, and problems; and identify and resolve potential policy tradeoffs before implementing the technology.

In the wake of the controversy over San Francisco Public Library's decision to adopt RFID, librarians Karen Schneider and Lori Ayre criticized libraries for implementing RFID without thoroughly examining the technology and its potential problems. Schneider urged librarians to undertake a searching review of RFID that emphasized protecting user privacy and security while providing for full disclosure and accountability on the part of the library.[20] Ayre argued that the library community needed to ensure that adoption of RFID was done in a manner consistent with established privacy principles, as libraries' use of RFID would serve to legitimize the use of the technology in the wider society.[21] Both authors urged librarians to develop best practices for library RFID applications that would model an ethical approach to RFID that preserves user privacy.

Privacy Guidelines and Consensus

In response to the appeals from privacy advocates and librarians concerned about RFID's impact on library users' privacy, ALA's Intellectual Freedom Committee (IFC) and Office for Information Technology Policy (OITP) committed to identifying key privacy issues associated with RFID and to work with interest groups concerned with influencing RFID privacy protections. ALA representatives began to work cooperatively with a task force convened by the Book Industry Study Group (BISG), a trade association representing groups involved in manufacturing, publishing, and distributing books. The task force's goals were to examine issues common to booksellers, manufacturers, and libraries and to draft privacy principles for use of RFID that would guide the use of RFID by BISG's members and associated organizations.[22]

In September 2004, the task force completed its work and published its privacy guidelines as BISG Policy Statement POL-02, *Radio Frequency Identification.* These policy principles required book industry groups to adopt and enforce a privacy policy that discloses the terms of use for data collected via RFID; ensure that no personal information is recorded on RFID tags (though the policy allows a variety of transactional data); protect data by reasonable security safeguards; comply with industry best practices and relevant federal, state, and local laws; and ensure that compliance with the four principles can be verified by an independent audit.[23]

The IFC and OITP incorporated these guidelines into the *Resolution on Radio Frequency Identification (RFID) Technology and Privacy Principles* and presented the resolution to the ALA Council for adoption as a first step in addressing the ethical concerns raised by libraries' use of RFID.[24] The resolution endorsed the BISG policy statement as a whole, adopted the specific privacy guidelines contained in the BISG policy statement, and mandated that ALA develop implementation guidelines for the use of RFID technologies in libraries. The ALA Council adopted the *Resolution on Radio Frequency Identification (RFID) Technology and Privacy Principles* at the ALA's 2005 Midwinter Meeting.[25]

As directed by the council resolution, the Intellectual Freedom Committee began to develop guidelines and best practices for the use of RFID in libraries.[26] During the process, the IFC solicited comments from ALA leaders and members to ensure that the guidelines would help libraries both to benefit from RFID deployment and to protect the privacy of library users. The final document, *RFID in Libraries: Privacy and Confidentiality Guidelines,* outlined policy guidelines for libraries adopting RFID. The document offered guidance on developing written privacy policies for implementing RFID in the library and identified several key best practices:

- Notify users about the library's use of RFID technology.
- Label all RFID tag readers clearly so users know they are in use.
- Protect the data on RFID tags by using encryption, if available.
- Limit the information stored on the RFID tag to a unique identifier or barcode.
- Block the public from searching the catalog by the unique identifier.
- Store no personally identifiable information on any RFID tag.[27]

ALA's adoption of privacy guidelines and best practices for RFID provided the library community with the tools it needed to address most of the concerns of privacy advocates and library users. The fundamental recommendations for libraries implementing RFID technology—providing notice, practicing transparency, limiting the information carried on the tag, and ensuring the security of the RFID application—are now a consensus baseline. Works providing guidance for librarians considering RFID recommend that libraries implementing RFID adopt policies consistent with the 2005 *Resolution on Radio Frequency Identification (RFID) Technology and Privacy Principles* and follow the recommendations outlined in the 2006 *RFID in Libraries: Privacy and Confidentiality Guidelines.*[28]

NISO Offers A New Model for RFID in Libraries

In December 2007, the National Information Standards Organization (NISO) issued *RFID in U.S. Libraries,* authored by a working group that included four RFID vendors, two software application providers, two librarians from libraries using RFID technology, and two consultants representing book industry related organizations. The publication sets forth NISO's "Recommended Practices" to facilitate the use of RFID in library applications. According to NISO, these recommended practices are intended to be a best practice or guideline for methods, materials, or practices used by an industry and are supposed to represent a leading-edge practice, an exceptional model, or a proven industry practice.

Viewed as a "best practice" or "guideline," *RFID in U.S. Libraries* is an unusual document. In addition to its primary goal of recommending standards and a data model to facilitate interoperability between different vendors' library RFID systems, the document offers a discussion of the benefits of RFID across the publishing supply chain. Libraries are regarded as one link in this "book publishing value chain," along with publishers, printers, manufacturers, distributors, wholesalers, retailers, and technology vendors. Consequently, the document recommends the adoption of a library RFID tag that can be used across the entire life cycle of a book or other library material, utilizing a data model that not only serves the needs of libraries, but also serves the needs of publishers, printers, wholesalers, jobbers, retailers, and even sellers of used books.[29]

As a result, the recommended data model includes fields for many optional data objects in addition to the mandatory primary identifier or barcode used by libraries. Among these are fields for the title of the work, an ISBN or UCC code, shelf location or call number, the supply chain stage, a supplier ID, order and invoice numbers, and supplier identification data. To ensure the future utility of the tag, the data model mandates that no controls be placed on any current or future use of these data fields, so that conceivably a book's RFID tag could provide information about the book's title, the owning library, and its bibliographic information, all without accessing the library's integrated library system (ILS).

The document also examines and assesses the privacy concerns associated with the use of RFID technologies. As a document intended to offer "best practices" for library RFID applications, its discussion of privacy issues is notable for what it does not contain:

- The document does not consider or discuss the unique privacy concerns of the U.S. library, which loans materials to patrons with a promise of confidentiality.
- It fails to reference the primary ALA statement addressing RFID implementation in libraries, *RFID in Libraries: Privacy and Confidentiality Guidelines*.
- It does not discuss fundamental recommendations such as the recommendation that libraries store only a unique identifier or barcode on the RFID tag in order to protect user privacy.

Instead, the document minimizes privacy issues associated with RFID as "mostly science fiction" and reprints, nearly verbatim, the VTLS-sponsored white paper published back in 2003 as a response to privacy advocates' concerns about RFID in the library.[30] The sole recommendation is that RFID tags comply with the privacy guidelines contained in *BISG Privacy Policy POL-002*, with an emphasis on the provision that no personal information is recorded on RFID tags.[31]

This lone recommendation is accompanied by a brief history of BISG Privacy Policy POL-002 that presents the BISG policy as the result of a joint ALA/BISG initiative and as the sole policy concerning privacy and RFID adopted by ALA. Internal ALA documents, such as reports from the ALA Intellectual Freedom Committee and the full text of the *Resolution on Radio Frequency Identification (RFID) Technology and Privacy Principles* provide a different account. These documents identify the policy as an initiative of the Book Industry Study Group and clarify that the endorsement of the BISG policy as a whole and the adoption of portions of the BISG policy were part of a larger effort that called for the development of specific RFID privacy guidelines for the library profession.[32]

As with the recommended data model, the privacy recommendations contained in *RFID in U.S. Libraries* reflect the needs of the commercial entities that make up the supply chain and not the needs and concerns of libraries and librarians. The minimal privacy standards recommended by the NISO document support commercial RFID applications that require greater amounts of data to be stored on the tag. Library-specific privacy standards that recommend limiting the data on the tag to a unique identifier, such as ALA's *RFID in Libraries: Privacy and Confidentiality Guidelines*, are neither considered nor included as a recommended practice because they are seen as a barrier to the adoption of an RFID tag that can be used across the publishing supply chain.

Conclusion

The discussion of privacy issues included in *RFID in U.S. Libraries* suggests that a deep divide exists between the library profession and the members of the working group responsible for drafting *RFID in U.S. Libraries*. The working group appears to not fully share librarians' concern about RFID's potential to invade library users' privacy, nor does it appear to accept librarians' own assessment of the role of libraries in society. As a result, the data models and recommended privacy practices promulgated for libraries look to future commercial use of RFID technologies by publishers, manufacturers, wholesalers, and retailers.

This result calls to mind the political and economic theory known as "regulatory capture," a model in which government regulation reflects the influence of special interests, and operates for their benefit.[33] The standards and privacy recommendations contained in RFID in U.S. Libraries reflect the influence of the vendors, software providers, and book industry advocates that dominate the working group, and appear to serve their interests at the expense of librarians' ethical concerns and obligations.

Librarians thus need to ask whether standards and best practices that regard libraries as part of a retail supply chain serve the best interests of libraries and their users. Libraries are not retail establishments, and librarians are not sales clerks. Rather, libraries are institutions whose mission is to serve the public good by making available information and ideas, and librarians are professionals who assure access to that information by defending the freedom to read and the right to privacy. Best practices for RFID in the library should not only facilitate use of the technology but also promote the library's distinctive mission and preserve users' privacy rights. They should not be compromised in order to serve the needs of vendors, manufacturers, wholesalers, retailers, and publishers, whose mission is to maximize profits on behalf of their shareholders.

Furthermore, librarians must ask whether recommended best practices for library RFID applications should look forward to uncertain future uses of RFID in the publishing supply chain, or address the present uses and known privacy and security vulnerabilities of library RFID tags. This inquiry is especially important given the publishing industry's slow adoption of RFID technology and libraries' increasing emphasis on e-books and other online media downloads that make no use of RFID. Standards and recommended practices can be revised and re-written to accommodate new RFID applications, but privacy, once lost, is not easily recovered.

In making these points, I do not mean to imply that librarians should not work with the book industry on establishing data models for library RFID applications or should forgo consideration of an RFID tag that can be used across various industries and organizations and permit interoperability between library RFID applications. Instead, librarians should assume a leadership role in developing best practices and standards for RFID, both inside and outside the library, as part of their ethical obligation to protect library users' privacy. Such standards should make privacy protection a primary goal, and not a secondary goal, when implementing RFID. This is especially important in the United States, where, with minor exceptions, there are no statutes or regulations that govern the use of RFID technologies.[34]

In a 2003 interview, librarian Karen Schneider eloquently summarized the challenge RFID poses for the library profession:

> What are we witness to as librarians? We have a chance here—not simply on behalf of library users and librarians, but also for society at large—to present an ethical approach to RFID and similar technologies, to actually present a framework for how to do this and preserve privacy in an increasingly non-private world. And conversely, if we don't develop best practices, I think we are acceding to an increasingly commercialized, non-private world and we're losing the opportunity to do something that we've done very

well, which is to find intellectual freedom and privacy issues in a particular technology and speak to them very clearly a way that the public can understand.[35]

Her concerns remain relevant today.

Notes

1. Lori Bowen Ayre, "Wireless Tracking in Libraries: Benefits, Threats, and Responsibilities," in RFID: Applications, Security, and Privacy, ed. Simson Garfinkel and Beth Rosenberg, 229–243 (Upper Saddle River, NJ: Addison-Wesley, 2005); Alan Butters, "RFID Systems, Standards, and Privacy within Libraries," The Electronic Library 25, no. 4 (2007): 430–439; David Molnar and David Wagner, "Privacy and Security in Library RFID Issues, Practices, and Architectures," in Proceedings of the 11th ACM Conference on Computer and Communications Security, ed. Birgit Pfitzmann and Peng Liu, 210–219 (New York: ACM, 2004).
2. Ayre, "Wireless Tracking in Libraries"; Laura Smart, "Considering RFID: Benefits, Limitations, and Best Practices," College and Research Library News 66, no. 1 (Jan. 2005): 13–16, 42.
3. Alan Butters, "Radio Frequency Identification: An Introduction for Library Professionals," Aplis 19, no. 4 (2006): 164–174.
4. Richard W. Boss, RFID Technology for Libraries, June 30, 2009. www.lita.org/ala/mgrps/divs/pla/plapublications/platechnotes/rfidtechnology.cfm (accessed Aug. 10, 2010); Karen Schneider, "RFID and Libraries: Both Sides of the Chip,"(testimony presented at the Committee on Energy and Utilities, California Senate, Nov. 19, 2003), www.ala.org/ala/aboutala/offices/oif/ifissues/rfidbothsideschip.pdf (accessed Sept. 14, 2010).
5. Boss, RFID Technology for Libraries.
6. Smart, "Considering RFID."
7. Electronic Frontier Foundation, "Statement to the San Francisco Library Commission," Oct. 1, 2003, www.eff.org/files/filenode/rfid/sfpl_comments_oct012003.pdf (accessed Sept. 14, 2010).
8. Alorie Gilbert, "California Probes RFID Technology," Globe and Mail, Aug. 11, 2003.
9. David Ewalt, "Wal-Mart Shelves RFID Experiment," Information Week, July 14, 2003.
10. Office for Intellectual Freedom, Intellectual Freedom Manual, 8th ed. (Chicago: American Library Association, 2010).
11. Vinod Chachra and Daniel McPherson, Personal Privacy and Use of RFID Technology in Libraries, Oct. 31, 2003, www.vtls.com/media/en-US/brochures/vtls_fastrac_privacy.pdf (accessed Sept. 14, 2010).
12. Boss, RFID Technology for Libraries; Butters, "RFID Systems, Standards, and Privacy within Libraries"; David Dornan, "Technically Speaking: RFID Poses No Problem for Patron Privacy," American Libraries, Dec. 2003: 86.
13. Walt Crawford, "Technology, Privacy, Confidentiality, and Security," in "Policy and Library Technology," Library Technology Reports 41, no. 2 (March–April 2005): 24–30;

Schneider, "RFID and Libraries"; Smart, "Considering RFID."
14. Ibid.
15. Molnar and Wagner, "Privacy and Security in Library RFID Issues"; Scott Muir, "RFID Security Concerns," Library Hi Tech 25, no. 1 (2007): 95–107.
16. Molnar and Wagner, "Privacy and Security in Library RFID Issues."
17. Butters, "RFID Systems, Standards, and Privacy within Libraries."
18. Butters, "Radio Frequency Identification"; Molnar and Wagner, "Privacy and Security in Library RFID Issues."
19. Smart, "Considering RFID."
20. Schneider, "RFID and Libraries."
21. Ayre, "Wireless Tracking in Libraries."
22. Office for Intellectual Freedom, Intellectual Freedom Manual.
23. Book Industry Study Group, Radio Frequency Identification, BISG Policy Statement POL-002, Sept. 2004, www.bisg.org/docs/BISG_Policy_002.pdf (accessed Sept. 14, 2010).
24. "History: RFID in Libraries: Privacy and Confidentiality Guidelines" in Intellectual Freedom Manual, Eighth Edition, compiled by the Office for Intellectual Freedom,288-292 (Chicago: American Library Association, 2010).
25. Ibid. at 289-90; see also "Resolution on Radio Frequency Identification (RFID) Technology and Privacy Principles," Jan. 19, 2005, www.ala.org/ala/aboutala/offices/oif/statementspols/ifresolutions/rfidresolution.cfm (accessed Sept. 19, 2010).
26. Ibid. at 291–292.
27. Ibid.; see also 284–287.
28. Connie K. Haley, Lynne A. Jacobsen, and Shai Robkin, Radio Frequency Identification Handbook for Librarians (Westport, CT: Libraries Unlimited, 2007); Diane Marie Ward, The Complete RFID Handbook (New York: Neal Schuman, 2007).
29. National Information Standards Organization, RFID in U.S. Libraries, NISO RP-6-2008, Dec. 2008, www.niso.org/apps/group_public/download.php/116/RP-6-2008.pdf (accessed Sept. 14, 2010).
30. Chachra and McPherson, "Personal Privacy and Use of RFID Technology;" NISO, RFID in U.S. Libraries, 37.
31. NISO, *RFID in U.S. Libraries*, viii, 37-40.
32. *Intellectual Freedom Manual*, 288-292.
33. Michael E. Levine and Jennifer Forrence, "Regulatory Capture, Public Interest, and the Public Agenda: A Synthesis," *Journal of Law, Economics, and Organization*, 6, special issue 1990, 167–198.
34. Thirteen states have adopted laws regulating RFID use in drivers' licenses and other identity documents and human implantation. Four states criminalize the unauthorized skimming of RFID-enabled identity cards if done for a criminal purpose. (See National Conference of State Legislatures, State Statutes Relating to Radio Frequency Identification (RFID) and Privacy, Sept. 2010, www.ncsl.org/default.aspx?tabid=13442n [accessed Sept.19, 2010].)
35. Gordon Flagg, "Should Libraries Play Tag with RFIDs?" (2003) *American Libraries*, December, 69–71.

About the Authors

Angela Maycock serves as assistant director of the Office for Intellectual Freedom at the American Library Association. She provides guidance and support to librarians, teachers, and others on the application of ALA's intellectual freedom policies and the First Amendment in specific situations involving materials challenges and confidentiality in the library. She also undertakes projects to educate librarians and the general public about intellectual freedom issues through speaking engagements, conference programming, and initiatives such as ALA's National Conversation on Privacy. Angela is passionate about connecting librarians with the resources they need to confront the complex challenges to intellectual freedom in libraries today. Prior to her work at ALA, Angela served as reference and instruction librarian at the Michigan State University Libraries. She received her MS in library science from the University of Illinois at Urbana-Champaign and her BA in English from Penn State University.

Barbara M. Jones is the director of the Office for Intellectual Freedom at the American Library Association. She received her PhD in U.S. history from the University of Minnesota and her MLS from Columbia University. She has spent most of her career as an academic librarian, her most recent post being university librarian at Wesleyan University in Connecticut. She has served on a number of intellectual freedom committees at ALA and recently was a member of the FAIFE Committee (Free Access to Information and Freedom of Expression) for the International Federation of Library Associations (IFLA). She has conducted training sessions on freedom of expression in Mexico, Costa Rica, Brazil, Nigeria, South Africa, Japan, and the Philippines. She has written extensively on the topic of intellectual freedom, her most recent book being *Protecting Intellectual Freedom in Your Academic Library*, published by ALA Editions in 2009.

Eli Neiburger is the associate director for IT and production at the Ann Arbor (Michigan) District Library, where he is responsible for software development, digitization, events and marketing. He is the author of *Gamers . . . in the LIBRARY?!"* (ALA Editions, 2007) and is working a new book titled *Did You Reboot IT? Inside and beyond the Library-IT Culture Wars*.

Sarah Houghton-Jan is the digital futures manager for the San José Public Library. Sarah writes the award-winning blog about library technology, *Librarian In Black*. She is also the author of the book *Technology Training in Libraries*. Sarah is a frequent consultant, speaker, and trainer on issues of libraries, technology, and user experience design. Sarah was named a 2009 *Library Journal* Mover and Shaker as a Trendspotter.

Jason Griffey is an associate professor and head of library information technology at the University of Tennessee at Chattanooga. His latest book, *Mobile Technology and Libraries*, is now available as a part of Neal Schuman's Tech Set. Jason's previous book, *Library Blogging*, with Karen A Coombs, is available through Amazon. He can be stalked obsessively at www.jasongriffey.net and at *Pattern Recognition*, his personal blog. He is the author of the *American Libraries Perpetual Beta* blog (http://bit.ly/perpetualbeta), and is also a columnist for the ALA Techsource blog (www.ts.ala.org/blogs/jason-griffey). Jason was named one of *Library Journal*'s Movers and Shakers in 2009 and is regularly invited to speak on libraries, the social economy, mobile technology, and other technology-related issues. He spends his free time with his daughter, Eliza, reading, obsessing over gadgets, and preparing for the inevitable zombie uprising.

Deborah Caldwell-Stone is deputy director of the American Library Association's Office for Intellectual Freedom, where she works on initiatives promoting the defense of the First Amendment freedom to read and the application of constitutional law to library policies, principles, and problems. An attorney by training, she now works closely with librarians, teachers, and library trustees on a wide range of intellectual freedom issues, including book challenges, Internet filtering, meeting room policies, and the impact of new technologies and the USA PATRIOT Act on library privacy and confidentiality. She is on the faculty of the ALA-sponsored Lawyers for Libraries and Law for Librarians workshops and speaks frequently to library groups around the country. Before she joined ALA in 2000, Deborah practiced appellate law before the state and federal courts in Chicago, Illinois. She earned her law degree with honors from Chicago-Kent College of Law at the Illinois Institute of Technology and is currently a student in the Graduate School of Library and Information Science's MSLIS program at the University of Illinois at Urbana-Champaign.

Notes

Library Technology Reports Respond to Your Library's Digital Dilemmas

Eight times per year, *Library Technology Reports* (LTR) provides library professionals with insightful elucidation, covering the technology and technological issues the library world grapples with on a daily basis in the information age.

\	*Library Technology Reports* 2010, Vol. 46
January 46:1	**"Understanding the Semantic Web: Bibliographic data and Metadata"** by Karen Coyle, Digital Library Consultant
February/ March 46:2	**"RDA Vocabularies for a 21st-Century Data Environment"** by Karen Coyle, Digital Library Consultant
April 46:3	**"Gadgets & Gizmos: Personal Electronics at your Library"** by Jason Griffey, Head of Library Information Technology, University of Tennessee at Chattanooga
May/June 46:4	**"Object Reuse and Exchange (OAI-ORE)"** by Michael Witt, Interdisciplinary Research Librarian & Assistant Professor of Library Science, Purdue University Libraries
July 46:5	**"Hope, Hype, and VoIP: Riding the Library Technology Cycle"** by Char Booth, E-Learning Librarian, University of California, Berkeley
August/ September 46:6	**"The Concept of Electronic Resource Usage and Libraries"** by Jill E. Grogg, E-Resources Librarian, University of Alabama Libraries, and Rachel A. Fleming-May, Assistant Professor, School of Information Sciences at the University of Tennessee
October 46:7	**"Rethinking Library Linking: Breathing New Life into OpenURL"** by Cindi Trainor, Coordinator for Library Technology & Data Services at Eastern Kentucky University, and Jason Price, E-resource Package Analyst, Statewide California Electronic Library Consortium
November/ December 46:8	**"Privacy and Freedom of Information in 21st-Century Libraries"** by the ALA Office for Intellectual Freedom, Chicago, IL

ALA TechSource

www.alatechsource.org

ALA TechSource, a unit of the publishing department of the American Library Association